✳

A BIBLIOGRAPHY OF
ARTHUR WALEY

✳

ARTHUR WALEY

FRANCIS A. JOHNS

✻

A BIBLIOGRAPHY OF
ARTHUR WALEY

✻

RUTGERS UNIVERSITY PRESS

New Brunswick   *New Jersey*

Copyright © 1968 by Rutgers, The State University
Library of Congress Catalog Card Number: 67-20388

*Manufactured in the United States of America
by Quinn & Boden Company, Inc., Rahway, N.J.*

A grant from the Asian Literature Program of The Asia Society, New York, made possible the publication of this book.

自伐者無功
自矜者不長

Prefatory Note

When I broached to Arthur Waley the matter of an introduction to this bibliography of his writings, he characteristically turned the suggestion aside with a comment recalling the words of T'ao Ch'ien which he himself translated: "To be untrue to myself could only lead to muddle." He would regard too a few of my requests for information as potential sources of muddle, and seemed amused that people might find meaningful some of the details expected by the users of bibliographies which even his many-sided mind had not considered. Such was his versatility that there would indeed be few people equipped to write comprehensively of the work of such a polymath as Waley. For these two reasons then it has seemed best to leave him to speak for himself, through this record of his work, to those interested in the diverse fields of which he was at once such a respected and such a graceful master. Though he has, for example, disclaimed having enriched English poetry —one poet even accused him of having harmed it extensively too—it has been said that a study of this aspect of his work is long overdue. A list of his writings may then be useful to investigators in many more areas than simply that of oriental studies, for Arthur Waley consistently and successfully refused to separate literature and learning.

No bibliographer can hope to give descriptions of such fullness as will meet completely the needs of all the various users of his work and still find a publisher. Some of the limitations accepted and conventions adopted are:

a) The technical collation for books has been omitted, as its presence in this case does not serve a really useful purpose.

b) Title-pages have been transcribed entire.

c) The height of a book in its original boards is given in centimetres.

d) The terms "impression" and "edition" have been used strictly.

e) Where it was ascertainable, the number of copies of a book printed is given in parentheses following the publication information. The figures were provided by publishers and can be assumed to give an idea of contemporary public interest.

f) Dr. Waley himself, in *The Life and Times of Po Chü-i*, mentions the value of recording the appearances of an author's work in anthologies. I agree with him and so have listed some representative ones, as well as the reprintings of books, translations into foreign languages, and musical settings of his work.

g) The aspirate has been rendered throughout as ' to facilitate the work of the printer.

F. A. J.

New Brunswick, New Jersey
June, 1966.

Contents

A. BOOKS

CHINESE POEMS

Confucius heard a boy singing:

" When the waters of the Ts'ang-lang are clear,
They do to wash my cap-tassels in.
When the waters of the Ts'ang-lang are muddy,
They do to wash my feet in."

PRINTED BY LOWE BROS.,
157, HIGH HOLBORN, LONDON W.C.

—

1916.

Chinese Poems, 1916. (13 x 20.5 cm)

A1 [*on cover*] CHINESE POEMS / [*ornament*] /
Confucius heard a boy singing: / "When the waters of
the Ts'ang-lang are clear, / They do to wash my cap-
tassels in. / When the waters of the Ts'ang-lang are
muddy, / They do to wash my feet in." / [*ornament*] /
PRINTED BY LOWE BROS., / 157 HIGH HOL-
BORN, LONDON W.C. / [*rule*] / 1916.

16 p. incl. covers.   20½ cm.

Contents, on ivory laid paper, within cover of the same
stock.

Privately printed for the translator.

Contents:

Notes:

The epigraph is from *Mencius*, IV, Pt. 1, Ch. viii, 2.

A.W. has said that about fifty copies were printed for distribution to friends, which doubtless explains why the collection nowhere bears his name. Rutgers University owns a notebook in which A.W. made a list of sixty-one people who were candidates to receive the work. Among the names are those of Lowes Dickinson, F. W. Bateson, Pound, Sickert, R. C. Trevelyan, Ricketts, Binyon, Squire, Fry, Eliot, B. Russell, Dulac, L. Woolf, Yeats, Helen Saunders, A. G. B. Russell, Logan Pearsall Smith, Dora Carrington, Sydney Cockerell, and Clive Bell. Copies belonging to the last five have been traced. In each of these copies there are some manuscript corrections, though not always the same ones in each copy. The wall-paper covers in which the booklets were sent out also vary from copy to copy.

A.W. tells the full story of the beginnings of the little book in his introduction to the second edition of 170 (**A2**).

The thirteen poems which were re-printed by A.W. (generally with changes) are identified by having the numbers of the books in which they subsequently appeared placed after them in the listing above. Where authorship attributions were changed, the later ones are given in square brackets. Only two of the poems translated seem to be later than the T'ang time.

An authorised facsimile reprint was made in 1965, with a brief preface, by F. A. Johns.

A2 A HUNDRED AND SEVENTY / CHINESE POEMS / TRANSLATED BY / ARTHUR WALEY / [*printer's flower*] / LONDON / CONSTABLE AND COMPANY LTD. / 1918

8vo. xii, 168 p.   20 cm.

Printed by Charles Whittingham and Co.   Tooks Court, Chancery Lane, London.

Drab paper boards, beige cloth spine. Lettered in brick-red on spine: 170 / *Chinese* / *Poems* / *Arthur* / *Waley* / [*at tail*] CONSTABLE / LONDON   Untrimmed.

Published July 1918, at 7/6.

Contents:

The notations in bold face following the individual
poems refer to the numbers of the entries in the bibliography which indicate the appearances of translations before publication in book form. These individual appearances
were often re-printed elsewhere with the same textual vari-
ations as the original (for a short list of some of these
periodicals, see Section B), before the book appeared. As
A.W. constantly revised his work, the latest state of a translation must be assumed to be the one which satisfied him
most.

An asterisk preceding a poem means that the Chinese
text as well as the translation may be found in *Select Chinese Verses* (A23).

Notes:

In his introduction to *More Translations* (A3), A.W. writes
concerning 170, ". . . no reviewer treated the book as an experi-
ment in unrhymed verse, though it was this aspect of it which
most interested the writer." For A.W.'s use of "sprung rhythm,"
see his "Notes on Translation" (C75), and the introduction to the
second edition of 170.

Authors' names given in square brackets are those attributed as
a result of later revisions by the translator. For the remarks of
H. A. Giles on the nine poems of the *Nineteen Old Poems* (No.
17) ascribed to Mei Shēng, see his "A Poet of the second century
B.C." in *New China Review*, 1920, p. 25–26.

An *errata* slip was tipped in before page v. A number of copies

(for review?) exist with the spine lettering in gold, and without
"170." Unfortunately records relating to the early publication of
the book are lost, and the verso of the title in later editions does
not agree with the information that Messrs. Constable were able
to supply. This latter has then been accepted as the more authorita-
tive and is tabulated below.

Impressions:

Second, (revised), 1918. Corrections on the *errata* slip were in-
corporated in the text, and p. [ii] bears the statement: *Second
Edition.*
Third, 1919.
Fourth, 1923.
Fifth, 1928. Added note on p. 17. Issued in *Constable's Mis-
cellany of original and selected publications in literature*, XII.
Sixth, 1932.
Seventh, Feb. 1936, 2150 copies.
Eighth, June 1939, 3000 copies.
Ninth, July 1942, 5000 copies.
Tenth, Nov. 1943, 2000 copies.
Eleventh, July 1945, 5000 copies.
Twelfth, Nov. 1946, 5000 copies.

Editions:

Second, Feb. 1962. A.W. substituted for the old one a new
introduction (dated 1960), in which he tells how he embarked
upon the study of Chinese. A few corrections are made to the
translations, and the bibliographical notes to the first edition are
dropped.
First American, May 1919, New York, A. A. Knopf, 1980 copies.
Second imp., Sept. 1919, 1530 copies.
Third imp., Mar. 1920, 997 copies.
Fourth imp., Dec. 1922, 1000 copies.
Fifth imp., Jan. 1935, 500 copies.
Sixth imp., Jan. 1938, 750 copies.

Popular Edition (Borzoi Pocket Books, A. A. Knopf), Feb. 1923.
  Second imp., Dec. 1923.
  Third imp.,   Feb. 1925.

Adaptations:

Bertolt Brecht, in his *Chinesische Gedichte*, 1939, based seven of his versions upon A.W.'s English translations: Nos. 15, 81, 82, 96, 101, 108 and 131 above. "The Big Rug" appeared again in the second tableau of *Der gute Mensch von Sezuan*.

Settings to music:

Blair Fairchild set Nos. 6, 8, 17 (7), 45, 54, 57, 60 and 119 to music for voice and piano in *Songs from the Chinese*, with French translation, Paris [1922].

Aaron Copland set No. 8 to music for high voice and piano in *Old Poem*, New York, 1923.

C. W. Orr set No. 60 to music for voice and piano in *Plucking the Rushes*, London, 1923.

Blair Fairchild set No. 17 (6) to music for voice and piano in *Le Message*, with French translation, Paris, 1928.

D. M. Stewart set Nos. 60 and 120 to music for voice and piano in *After Lunch* and *Plucking the Rushes*, London, 1929.

Freda Swain set No. 82 to music for voice and piano in *Experience*, London, 1931.

Among other (unpublished?) settings of poems from 170 are those by Freda Swain (1921–23), Denis ApIvor (1940) and Susan D'Arcy Clark (1942). For further settings of pieces first published in 170, see **A30**.

A3 MORE TRANSLATIONS / FROM THE CHINESE / BY / ARTHUR WALEY / AUTHOR OF "170 CHINESE POEMS" / [*device*] / LONDON:

GEORGE ALLEN & UNWIN LTD. / RUSKIN
HOUSE, 40 MUSEUM STREET, W.C. I [1919]

8vo. 109 p. 1l.   18½ cm.

Blue paper boards, white canvas spine. Lettered in blue
down spine: MORE TRANSLATIONS FROM THE
CHINESE. All edges trimmed.

Published July 1919, at 4/6.   (1428)

Contents:

p.   5–6   Introduction.
     11–107   Text.
     109   Appendix [*Bibliographical note*], followed by
              blank leaf.

The notations in bold face following the individual pieces refer to the numbers of the entries in the bibliography which indicate the appearance of translations before publication in book form.

Notes:

A.W. observes in the Introduction that he has aimed more consistently at poetic form in *More Translations* than he did in 170.

All the pieces here except Nos. 2, 3–5, 7, 10, 33, 60, 63, 65 and 68 are to be found in *Chinese Poems* (A30), and all, except No. 57, are in *Translations* . . . (A28).

Copies (of all three impressions) were also issued in ivory paper covers at 3/–. A binding-up, in glazed blue cloth with black lettering, of the third impression at least, is also to be found.

Musical settings of seven pieces first published in *More Translations* are recorded in the entry for *Chinese Poems* (A30).

Impressions:

Second, June 1920, 1250 copies.
Third,   1937.

Edition:

New York, Knopf, 1919, 3300 copies, including a *de luxe* issue.
Second imp.   1937, 2000 copies.

A4 [*on cover*] THE POET LI PO / A.D. 701–762 / BY ARTHUR WALEY / [*rule*] / A *Paper read before the* CHINA SOCIETY *at the School of Oriental Studies* / *on November* 21, 1918 / [*rule*] / EAST AND WEST, LTD. / 3, VICTORIA STREET, LONDON, S.W. 1 / 1919

29 p. 1l.   24 cm.

Printed by Billing and Sons, Ltd. Guildford.
Stapled within orange paper cover, back blank. All edges
trimmed.

Published Oct. 1919 at 2/–.

Contents:

XX, 8	Going down Chung-nan Mountain and spending the night drinking with the hermit Tou-ssŭ.
†*XXIII, 3	Drinking alone by moonlight.
*XXIII, 9	In the mountains on a summer day.
XXIII, 10	Drinking together in the mountains.
†*XXIII, 10	Waking from drunkenness on a spring day.
*XXIII, 13	Self-abandonment.
†*XXV, 1	To Tan Ch'iu.
*XXX, 8	Clearing up at dawn.
28–29	Discussion on the foregoing paper.
[31]	Printer's statement, verso blank.

Notes:

The numbering of the poems is that of the 1908 reprint of the Wang Ch'i edition of 1759. Pieces marked * were printed in *More Translations* . . . (A3), and those marked † in *The Poetry and Career of Li Po* (A33).

The paper was also printed in *The Asiatic Review*, Vol. XV, Oct. 1919, p. 584–610 (C7).

A5 JAPANESE POETRY / THE 'UTA' / BY / ARTHUR WALEY / ASSSISTANT IN THE BRITISH MUSEUM / OXFORD / AT THE CLARENDON PRESS / 1919

8vo. 110 p. 1l. front.   20 x 16 cm.

Printed at the Oxford University Press.

Sewn in grey paper covers lettered in blue as the title-page, with the addition, before the date, of the following: LONDON EDINBURGH GLASGOW NEW YORK / TORONTO MELBOURNE CAPE TOWN BOMBAY / HUMPHREY MILFORD /   Edges cut flush.

Published Oct. 31, 1919, at 6/– (1000?)

Contents:

Notes:

The text of the poems is in Japanese (Roman script) and English. The numbering of the poems in the various collections is as follows:

Manyō: 106, 107, 122, 223, 276, 309, 350, 354, 349, 361, 365, 378, 440, 452, 461, 486, 604, 632, 660, 665, 687, 691, 698, 741, 744, 778, 905, 979, 1001 *, 1014, 1063, 1089, 1129, 1150, 1179, 1251, 1252, 1289, 1291, 1369, 1426, 1500, 1663, 1666, 1791, 1879*, 1983, 2103, 2330, 2375, 2401, 2578, 2602, 3222*, 3244, 3332*, 4209*, 3669 of the 4173 tanka and 324 naga-uta in the collection.

Kokin: 131, 147, 156, 158, 169, 229, 411, 481, 493, 504, 517, 525, 542, 548, 560, 591, 601, 611, 624, 632, 637, 701, 747, 797, 838, 861, 895, 919, 928, 948, 961 of 1111 poems.

Gosen: 86, 146, 209, 322, 454*, 631*, 1196, 1307*, of 1426 poems.

Shū-i: 2*, 10*, 62*, 71*, 131*, 171, 184*, 190*, 202*, 223, 224*, 258*, 488*, 565*, 622*, 833, 848, 990, 1008, 1055, 1322, 1327, 1329*, 1331*, 1342* of 1351 poems.

Go-Jūi: 71*, 273, 382, 411.

Shikwa: 74, 156.

Senzai: 122, 463, 656, 916.

Shin Kokin: 88, 382, 449, 707, 1448.

Shin Chokusen: 23.

Gyokuyō: 2198.

Zoku Sensai: 397.

Rōyei: p. 8, 28, 47, 99, 170, 171.

Seven poems by Saigyo Hōshi.

Poems marked with an asterisk were revised in 1926, for inclusion, with parts of the Introduction, in the anthology *Lotus and Chrysanthemum,* 1927 (*q.v.* **G1**), in which were also re-printed fifty more Japanese poems first published in 1921 (**B21**).

"The translations in this book are chiefly intended to facilitate the study of the Japanese text . . . I have given this book the perhaps too comprehensive title 'Japanese Poetry,' but have excluded from it both the *hokku* and the poetry of the *Nō* Plays, hoping to deal later with both these subjects. The 'uta' of the sub-title means, of course, the 'uta' *par excellence*, that is to say, the verse of thirty-one syllables." (Introduction, p. 8) A.W.'s book, *The Nō Plays . . .* appeared in 1921 (**A6**, *q.v.*).

Tetsuzo Okada, in an article, "English Translations of the Manyōshū," in *Studies in English Literature*, Tokyo, Vol. XIII, No. 4, Oct. 1934, p. 468–81, gives the following revised authorship ascriptions for some of the pieces translated by A.W.:

Manyō Nos.:	106	Oku.
	354	Heki no O-oyu.
	452	Ōtomo no Tabito.
	461	Lady Sakanoye.
	604	Kasa no Iratsume.
	1014	Tachibana no Ayanavi.
	1063	Sakimaro.
	1089	Anon.

1879 Anon.
1983 Anon.
2103 Anon.
2230 Anon.
2578 Anon.
4209 Kume no Hironiwa.

He corrects a misprint—2203 for 2103—and adds a comment on No. 1791.

Sheets bound in mustard-colour cloth boards were made available in February 1920 at 7/6.

Impressions:

Second, 1946.
Third, 1956.
Fourth, 1959.
All these re-printings were produced by offset, using sheets of the original edition, and issued by Lund, Humphries Ltd.

Settings to music:

Solon Alberti set A.W.'s translations of *Manyō* Nos. 744 and 778, and *Kokin* Nos. 158 and 525 to music for voice and piano in *Four sketches from the Far East*, New York, 1938.

A6 THE NŌ PLAYS OF / JAPAN / BY / ARTHUR WALEY / WITH LETTERS BY OSWALD SICKERT / [*device*] / LONDON: GEORGE ALLEN & UNWIN LTD. / RUSKIN HOUSE, 40 MUSEUM STREET, W.C. 1. [1921]

8vo. 319 p. front. and 1 pl.   22½ cm.

Printed by Unwin Brothers, Limited   Woking and London

Yellow glazed cloth boards. White paper label on spine
reads: THE / NŌ PLAYS / OF JAPAN / * / AR-
THUR WALEY   Top edge trimmed.

Published March 1921, at 18/–. (1500)

Contents:

Seami
  Atsumori.
Komparu Zembō Motoyasu
  Ikuta.
Seami [Anon.]
  Tsunemasa.
Zenchiku Ujinobu [Anon.]
  Kumasaka.
Miyamasu
  Eboshi-ori.
Hiyoshi Sa-ami Yasukiyo [Anon.]
  Benkei on the bridge (Hashi-Benkei).

Seami
  Kagekiyo.
  Hachi no Ki.
Kwanami
  Sotoba Komachi.
Enami no Sayemon
  Ukai (The cormorant fisher).
Seami
  Aya no Tsuzumi (The damask drum).
Zenchiku Ujinobu [?]
  Aoi no Uye (Princess Hollyhock).
Authorship doubtful [Seami?]
  Kantan.
Zenchiku Ujinobu [Migamasu?]
  The Hōka priests (Hōkazō).
Seami [Anon.]
  Hagoromo.
Zenchiku Ujinobu
  Tanikō (The valley-hurling).
Seami
  Ikeniye (The pool-sacrifice).
Komparu Zembō Motoyasu
  Hatsuyuki (Early snow).
Seami
  Haku Rakuten.

Summaries of:
Seami
  Izutsu.
  Kakitsubata.
  Ominameshi.
  Shunkwan.

Ama (The fisher-girl).
Take no Yuki (Snow on the Bamboos).
Hotoke no Hara.
Kwanami (rev. by Seami)
Hanakatami (The flower basket).
Matsukaze.
Kongō Yagorō
Tori-oi.
I-ami
Tango-monogurui.
Komparu Zembō Motoyasu
Ikaku Sennin (The one-horned rishi).
Seami (rev. Zenchiku) [?]
Yamuba (The dame of the mountains).
Unknown author
Mari (The football).
Seami or Kwanami
Tōru.
Miyamasu
Mai-guruma (The dance-waggons).
Unknown author
The bird-catcher in hell (Esashi Jū-ō, one of the farcical
   parodies of Nō plays, or Kyōgen).

Revised authorship ascriptions in accordance with later
research are given in brackets following those assigned by
A.W.

Notes:

Dedicated, p. [2], "TO DŌAMI."

A.W. in his introduction, gives copious illustrative extracts from the *Works* of Seami, a manuscript of which was recovered in 1908.

The letters of Oswald Sickert, extracts from which are given in Appendix I, were written to Charles Ricketts in 1916.

Hagoromo, Ikeniye and *Hachi no Ki* (v. **B17**) *Hatsuyuki* (v. **B19**) and a passage from *Hōkazō* (v. **B20**) had all been published by A.W. before the appearance of *The Nō Plays*.

For other articles by A.W. referring to Nō, see **C13, C14** and **C26**.

Bertolt Brecht's play *Der Jasager* (1930) was adapted from A.W.'s translation of *Tanikō*. Brecht later revised the play and called it *Der Neinsager*. Both texts are available in Brecht's *Versuche 4*, and *Stücke IV*. See J. Willett, *The Theatre of Bertolt Brecht*, 1959, p. 36–37.

For the influence of *The Nō Plays*, and notably "Atsumori," on Jean Schlumberger's story *Stéphane le Glorieux*, 1940, see his *Œuvres*, T. VI, Paris, 1960, p. 9–11 and also a note by him in *La Nouvelle Revue Française*, Vol. XIX, 1922, p. 375–79, reviewing *The Nō Plays*.

Impressions:

Second, July 1950, 1500 copies.
Third, Nov. 1954, 2000 copies.
Fourth,   1965.
New York, Grove Press, Feb. 1957, 3500 copies (without the plates).

Edition:

New York, Knopf, March 1922, 2000 copies. An abbreviated introduction, six additional plates, no index.

Translation:

"Les Nō japonais par Arthur Waley, (Extraits). Traduction de Suzanne Bing" in *Jeux, tréteaux et personnages* [Auxerre, Yonne], No. 91, 15 July 1939, p. 199–224.

Incomplete translation of parts of the preface and introduction. Though the translator intended to continue publishing her work, the periodical appears to have suspended publication, doubtless due to the war, before any more extracts could be printed.

A7 AN INDEX OF / CHINESE ARTISTS / REPRESENTED IN THE SUB-DEPARTMENT / OF ORIENTAL PRINTS AND DRAWINGS / IN THE / BRITISH MUSEUM / BY / ARTHUR WALEY / ASSISTANT IN THE SUB-DEPARTMENT / PRINTED BY ORDER OF THE TRUSTEES / *SOLD AT THE BRITISH MUSEUM* / AND BY / MESSRS. LONGMANS & CO., 39 Paternoster Row; / BERNARD QUARITCH, LTD., 11 Grafton Street, New Bond Street; / HUMPHREY MILFORD, OXFORD UNIVERSITY PRESS, Amen Corner. / 1922 / [*All rights reserved*]

8vo. xii, 112 p.   21½ cm.

Printed by Stephen Austin and Sons, Ltd., Hertford.

Grey paper boards, with upper cover printed in black, within a triple rule, as the title-page. All edges trimmed, and boards cut flush.

Published March 1922, at 15/–. (300)

Contents:

p.	v–vi	Preface, by Laurence Binyon.
	vii–xii	Introduction.
	1–112	Text.
	112	Errata.

Notes:

The *Index* includes the names, not only of those artists whose original work was then available in the department, but also of those whose work was present in reproduction. A.W. gives, in his introduction, a list of books, journals and catalogues in Eastern and Western languages, the contents of which are included. Certain collections of photographs were also incorporated. Laurence Binyon says further: "a certain number of artists have been inserted who are not represented in the Museum collection but whose names occur in notices of other artists." Cross-references from *ming, tzŭ* and *hao* are provided as well as brief biographical notes and references. The following two articles by W. Speiser complement the *Index:*

"Ergänzungen zu Waley's Index" in *Ostasiatische Zeitschrift,* Vol. 17, 1931, p. 124–29.

"Weitere Ergänzungen zu Waley's Index" in *Ost. Zeit.,* Vol. 24, 1938, p. 230–39.

A8   ZEN BUDDHISM / and Its Relation to Art / By / ARTHUR WALEY / LONDON: / LUZAC & CO., 46, Great Russell Street, W.C. 1 / 1922

31 p.   21½ cm.

Printed by The Utopia Press, 44 Worship Street, London, E.C. 2.

Stapled within stiff yellow paper covers, white on inside, lettered as the title-page. Edges trimmed.

Published April 1922, at 2/6.

Contents:

Note:

"This paper is intended for ordinary people, not for sinologues or specialists in Buddhism. . . . Students of art will perhaps be interested by the fresh light which I have been able to throw upon the careers of Mokkei [Mu-chi] and Mokuan." p. [5]

Most of the paper is contained in Chapter XVII of *An Introduction to the study of Chinese Painting* (A9, *q.v.*)

Impressions:

Another impression, in grey paper covers, was produced, by offset methods, in 1959.

A9   AN INTRODUCTION TO THE STUDY OF / CHINESE PAINTING / BY ARTHUR WALEY / ASSISTANT IN THE BRITISH MUSEUM / [*device*] / MCMXXIII / LONDON: ERNEST BENN, LIMITED / 8, BOUVERIE STREET, E.C. 4

8vo. 2l, xii, 261 p. 1l.   front. (col.) and 48 pl. (5 col.)   28½ cm.

Printed by William Brendon and Son, Ltd., The Mayflower Press, Plymouth.

Fawn buckram-covered bevelled boards, lettered on spine in gold: AN / INTRODUCTION / TO THE / STUDY OF / CHINESE / PAINTING / WALEY / [*at tail*] BENN   Edges trimmed. Top stained fawn.

Published Sept. 1923, at 3½ gns. (800 and 250 for Scribner)

Contents:

Lu T'an-wei, Hsieh Ho.

Chapter VII. The Six Dynasties: the Wei Tartars and their art.

The rock sculptures of Yün-kang, Tun-huang, The South, The Korean tomb-paintings, Chang Sēng-yu, Ts'ao Chung-ta, The Sui dynasty.

Chapter VIII. The T'ang dynasty.

The Spell of Vaiśravana, The middle period, T'ang poetry, The fall of Ming Huang, Late T'ang.

Chapter IX. The T'ang painters.

Buddhist art; Wu Tao-tzŭ and his followers, Yen Li-tē and Yen Li-pēn, Wu Tao-tzŭ, Wu's style, Wu's pupils, Wu's influence upon sculpture, Later Buddhist painting.

Chapter X. The Tun-huang paintings.

The Hōryūji wall-paintings, The Stein collection, The piety of Tun-huang, The Tun-huang paintings an archaic provincial school, The Kwako Genzai Ingwa Kyō.

Chapter XI. Landscape painting.

Li Ssŭ-hsün: Wang Wei and monochrome painting, Wang Wei's career, Monochrome painting, Wang Wei's pictures, Final development of ink technique.

Chapter XII. Animals, Birds and Flowers.

The animal painters, Flower-painting, Court scenes, Art criticism in the T'ang dynasty.

Notes:

Dedicated to Laurence Binyon.
A.W. himself warns the reader in Chapter I: "This book is
rather a series of essays than a general survey of early Chinese

painting . . . . I have confined myself, so far as possible to topics of which I have special knowledge." (p. 3)

Chapter XVII had previously appeared, in slightly expanded form, as a separate paper, *Zen Buddhism and its relation to Art* (A8, *q.v.*).

Some noteworthy translations in the book follow:

Ts'ao Chih	The Lo-Shēn poem [*Excerpt*]	p. 60–62
Shēn Yo	Wild geese	p. 109
Wang Wei	Picnics [*Two pieces*]	p. 141–42
Chu Kuang-hsi	The herdboy	p. 156–57
Su Tung-p'o	Mount Lu	p. 177

The second and third poems appear in *Poems from the Chinese,* 1927 (A14); the others do not seem to be included elsewhere in A.W.'s writings.

Impressions:

Fifty *de luxe* copies of the first impression exist, bound in pig-skin, printed on hand-made paper and signed by the author. Two hundred and fifty copies, bearing the imprint of Charles Scribner's Sons, were exported for sale in the United States.

A second impression of 2000 copies was produced by Grove Press of New York using offset methods (except for the coloured plates), and re-issued in April 1958. The sheets for England bear the Ernest Benn imprint.

A10 THE TEMPLE / AND OTHER POEMS / TRANSLATED BY / ARTHUR WALEY / WITH AN / INTRODUCTORY ESSAY ON / EARLY CHINESE POETRY, AND AN / APPENDIX ON THE DEVELOPMENT / OF DIFFERENT MET-RICAL FORMS / LONDON: GEORGE ALLEN

& UNWIN LTD. / RUSKIN HOUSE, 40 MUSEUM STREET, W.C. 1 [1923]

8vo. 1l. 150, [I] p. 1l.   20 cm.

Printed by Unwin Brothers Ltd, Woking and London.

Glazed yellow cloth boards. White paper spine label printed in blue reads: [*double rule*] / The / Temple / And Other / Poems / [*printer's flower*] / Arthur / Waley / [*double rule*]   Top edge trimmed.

Published Oct. 1923, at 6/–. (1180 and 520 for Knopf)

Contents:

p.   9–61   Introduction. Chapter I.
                 The Odes, Literary Poetry, The Metrical Form of the *Fu*, Origins of the *Fu*, Other Poems of Ch'ü Yüan.
                 1. The Nine Hymns [*with extracts*]. 2. The Heavenly Questionings. 3. The Nine Declarations. 4. The Distant Wandering. 5. Consulting the Soothsayer. 6. Dialogue with a Fisherman. 7. The Great Summons [*More Translations* No. 1].
                 Sung Yü, 1. The Summons to the Soul. 2–10. The Nine Changes [*with extract*]. 11. Sung Yü's Defence [*in extenso*]. 12. Big Words [*with extract*]. 13. Little Words [*with extract*]. 14. Master Teng-t'u [*part*, No. 3 in 170]. 15. The Wind [No. 2 in 170]. 16. Kao T'ang [No. 1 *infra*]. 17. The Goddess. 18. The Flute.

Chapter II.

The Ch'in Empire. The Princess. Tsou Yang. Mei Shēng [*extracts from 'The Seven Incitements'*]. Ssŭ-ma Hsiang-ju [*with extract*].

Chapter III.

Yang Hsiung, Chang Hēng, Wang I and Wang Yen-shou, Shu Hsi, T'ao Ch'ien [*text of 'Dirge on his own Death'*].

Chapter IV.

Later history of the *Fu*, Ballads, *The Temple*.

63–133 Text.

Ballad

137–46   Appendix I. The Forms of Chinese Poetry.
           Development of the three regular metres.
           T'ien-tz'ŭ or Filled-out Verse [*Li Hou-*
           chu's 'Immeasurable Pain' given as an
           example]
147–48   Appendix II. Texts [*Sources of the transla-*
           tions]
149–[51]   Index.
           One blank leaf.
           The notations in bold face following the
           individual poems refer to the numbers of the
           entries in the bibliography which indicate
           the appearances of translations before pub-
           lication in book form.

Notes:

Dedicated to: MR. F.-D. AND B., ESQ.
". . . I would point out that they [*the translations*] are all
meant to be read out loud. They cease to be metrical at all if only
scanned with the eye." (Introduction, p. 61)
A.W. says elsewhere (**C61**) that "The Bones of Chuang Tzu" is
"to my mind the finest of all long Chinese poems." He published
further work on *The Nine Hymns*, with a translation of Nos. 1–9
and 11 in *The Nine Songs*, 1955 (**A35**). No. 10 appears as the
first piece of 170 (**A2**).

Impression:

Second, Sept. 1925, 516 copies and 300 for A. A. Knopf, who was the distributor in the United States.

All THE TALE OF GENJI / BY / LADY MURA-SAKI / TRANSLATED FROM THE JAPANESE / BY / ARTHUR WALEY / *Est-ce vous, mon prince? lui dit-elle. Vous* / *vous êtes bien fait attendre!* / LONDON: GEORGE ALLEN & UNWIN LTD. / RUSKIN HOUSE, 40 MUSEUM STREET, W.C. 1 [1925]

8vo. 300 p. 2l.   22 cm.

Printed by Unwin Brothers Ltd, London and Woking.

Dark blue cloth boards, lettered in gold on spine: [*double rule*] / THE TALE / OF GENJI / By LADY / MURASAKI / [*leaf*] / ARTHUR / WALEY/ [*at tail*] GEORGE ALLEN / & UNWIN L^{TD} / [*double rule*]   Trimmed head and tail.

Published May 1925, at 10/6. (1508 and 1050 for Houghton Mifflin)

Contents:

Notes:

Dedicated to Beryl de Zoete, p. [5].

"My translation will probably occupy six volumes. In a seventh I shall translate the authoress's Diary (Murasaki Shikibu Nikki), discuss her position as a writer and give some particulars about the age in which she lived." (Preface) The proposed final volume did not appear, but see A.W.'s introductions to subsequent volumes.

The epigraph is taken from *La Belle au Bois Dormant* in Per-rault's *Contes de ma Mère l'Oye*.

The kind of difficulties which the translator had to overcome are well set forth in a brief article by Ivan Morris: "Translating 'The Tale of Genji,' " in *Orient/West*, Jan.–Feb. 1964, p. 21–24.

Impressions:

Sheets provided with the Houghton Mifflin imprint were ex-ported for issue in the United States after binding. Printing runs were as follows:

Second,	Aug. 1925,	500 copies and	2,100 for HM.
Third,	Nov. 1925,		2,044 for HM.
Fourth,	July 1926,	1,262 copies.	
Fifth,	Dec. 1927,	720 copies and	500 for HM.
Sixth,	Nov. 1932,	1,012 copies and	250 for HM.
Seventh,	May 1934,	810 copies and	500 for HM.
Eighth,	May 1935,	810 copies and	500 for HM.

Edition:

New York, Doubleday, June 1955, 20,000 copies. Lacks the two appendices present in the original edition and contains, as its

introduction, the material which constituted the introduction to
the original edition of Vol. III (**A13**).

Translations:

>Stockholm, Natur och Kultur, 1927.
>Paris, Plon, 1928.
>Amsterdam, Van Holkema and Warendorf, 1930.

Collected edition:

The publication history of the collected edition, which brings
together the text of the six parts under the title *The Tale of Genji,*
seems to be as follows:

Sept. 1935 Houghton Mifflin published a two-volume edition of 7,000 copies.

Nov. 1935 A further 3,100 sheets of the first printing, con-
stituting the English edition, were published
under the imprint of Allen and Unwin, who
issued them bound in one volume as well as
in two.

Mar. 1951 Allen and Unwin issued a photo-offset impression, in two volumes, consisting of 3,600
copies.

May 1957 The same publishers issued, this time in one
volume, a further impression of 3,840 copies.

1960 Random House, New York, produced, using the
Houghton Mifflin plates, a further 15,000
copies.

1965 Another, fourth, impression by Allen and Unwin.

Collected edition in translation:

Wiesbaden, Insel, 1937.
Turin, Einaudi, 1957.

Partial edition:

The Literary Guild, New York, printed the first four parts under the title *The Tale of Genji* in 1935.

Dramatisation:

Prince Genji, a play in three acts, London, 1960, by William Cooper (i.e., H. S. Hoff), owes its inspiration to A.W.'s translation of the novel. The play was broadcast by the BBC on March 6, 1950, and was first performed in Oxford in 1959.

A12   THE SACRED TREE / BEING THE SEC-OND PART / OF "THE TALE OF GENJI" / TRANSLATED FROM THE JAPANESE / BY / ARTHUR WALEY / LONDON: GEORGE ALLEN & UNWIN LTD / RUSKIN HOUSE, 40 MUSEUM STREET, W.C. 1 [1926]

8vo. 304 p.   22 cm.

Printed by Unwin Brothers Ltd, London and Woking.

Binding uniform with **A11**. Lettering uniform, except title, which reads: THE / SACRED /TREE   Top and bottom edges trimmed.

Published 23 Feb. 1926, at 10/6. (1424 and 5100 for Houghton Mifflin)

Contents:

p. [5]   Preface.
    13–14   Summary of Volume I.

Note:

Dedicated to Mary MacCarthy (née Warre-Cornish), p. [4].

Impressions:

Second, Feb. 1927, 760 copies.
Third, May 1933, 760 copies.

Editions:

Doubleday, Oct. 1959, 20,000 copies, lacking the Introduction
and Note on the text.

A13 A WREATH OF CLOUD / BEING THE
THIRD PART OF / "THE TALE OF GENJI" /
TRANSLATED FROM THE JAPANESE / BY /
ARTHUR WALEY / LONDON: GEORGE ALLEN
AND UNWIN LTD. / RUSKIN HOUSE, 40 MU-
SEUM STREET, W.C. 1 [1927]

8vo. 312 p.   22 cm.

Printed by Unwin Brothers Ltd, Woking.

Binding uniform with **A11**. Lettering uniform, except title, which reads: A WREATH / OF CLOUD Top and bottom edges trimmed.

Published 8 Feb. 1927 at 10/6. (1478 and 2522 for Houghton Mifflin)

Contents:

Note:

Dedicated to Raymond Mortimer, p. [5].

Impressions:

Second, Oct. 1928,   990 copies
           1937,   500 copies (Destroyed by enemy action)

A14 [*on cover, within a double rule, a border of printer's flowers and a single rule*] THE AUGUSTAN BOOKS OF / ENGLISH POETRY / SECOND SERIES NUMBER SEVEN / [*rule*] / ARTHUR / WALEY / (POEMS FROM THE / CHINESE) /

[*rule*] / *LONDON: ERNEST BENN LTD. / BOU-VERIE HOUSE, FLEET STREET* [1927]

31 p. incl. covers.   22 cm.

Printed by Billing and Sons, Ltd., Guildford and Esher.

Contents stapled within white paper cover. On back, list of the Augustan Books of Poetry.

Published Oct. 1927, at 6d.

Contents:

p. iii   Introduction by Humbert Woolf.
         The thirty-four translations are all contained in four
            of A.W.'s earlier books, as follows:
            170. Nos. 6, 9, 19, 54, 60, 68, 79, 84, 85, 90, 123,
               141.
            More translations. Nos. 7, 8, 33, 49, 50, 56, 57,
               60, 62, 65.
            The Temple. Nos. 4, 5, 6, 7, 10, 11 and p. 144.
            An Introduction . . . p. 14, 15, 16, 109, 141–42.

Notes:

   After complimentary remarks concerning the translations, Humbert Woolf says in his introduction: ". . . we must address ourselves to these poems as though they had been written by an Englishman of the twentieth century, and judge them on that basis."

A15 BLUE TROUSERS / BEING THE FOURTH PART OF / "THE TALE OF GENJI" / BY / LADY MURASAKI / TRANSLATED FROM THE JAP-

ANESE BY / ARTHUR WALEY / GEORGE
ALLEN & UNWIN LTD. / MUSEUM STREET
[1928]

8vo. 333 p. 1l.   22 cm.

Printed by Unwin Brothers Ltd, Woking.

Binding uniform with **A11**. Lettering uniform, title
reads: BLUE / TROUSERS   Top and bottom
edges trimmed.

Published May, 1928 at 10/6. (1630 and 2080 for
Houghton Mifflin)

Contents:

p.   11   Situation at the beginning of Volume IV.
    13–333   Text. [Chapters 29–40]
    [334]–[35] Advertisements.

Notes:

Dedicated to R. C. Trevelyan, p. [5].
Blue Trousers ends with the death of Genji. Volumes V and VI
contain the "ten Uji chapters" dealing with the fortunes of the
descendents of Genji.

Impressions:

Second, April, 1933, 1000 copies (printed in 1928).

A16   THE PILLOW-BOOK OF / SEI SHŌNAGON
/ TRANSLATED BY / ARTHUR WALEY /

LONDON / GEORGE ALLEN & UNWIN LTD /
MUSEUM STREET [1928]

8vo. 162 p. 1l.   20½ cm.

Printed by Unwin Brothers Ltd., Woking.

Wine-coloured cloth boards. Greyish-green cloth label
on spine, on which is lettered in gold: THE / PILLOW-
/ BOOK OF / SEI / SHŌNAGON / * / WALEY
Top edge trimmed.

Published Oct. 1928, at 6/–. (1500 and 1040 for
Houghton Mifflin)

Contents:

p.   5–6   Preliminary Notes.
      7–160   Text.
      161–62 Table to facilitate comparison with the orig-
              inal.
              One leaf of advertisements of other A.W.
              translations.

Notes:

Dedicated to Hazel Crompton, p. [2].
A.W. says that he has translated about a quarter of the *Makura
no Sōshi*, gives information concerning other translations of it and
cites the text that he used (Preliminary Notes, p. 5–6). The first
part of the book, until the end of page 19, consists of a brief introduction to tenth century Japan.

Impressions:

Second, July 1931, 1512 copies and 350 for HM.
Third,   1949, 2000 copies.

Fourth, April 1957, 1750 copies.
New York, Grove Press, Oct. 1960, 5000 copies.

Edition:

Second, Unwin Books, Nov. 1960. Contains brief preface, p. [5], dated Feb. 1960; lacks the Table.

A17 THE ORIGINALITY OF / JAPANESE / CIVILIZATION / *By* ARTHUR WALEY / OXFORD UNIVERSITY PRESS / LONDON: HUMPHREY MILFORD / 1929

15 p.   19 cm.

Printed by John Johnson, at the University Press, Oxford.

Stiff, cream-coloured, paper covers printed in blue: THE ORIGINALITY OF / JAPANESE / CIVILIZATION / *By* ARTHUR WALEY /   MCMXXIX / OXFORD UNIVERSITY PRESS / LONDON: HUMPHREY MILFORD   All edges trimmed, covers cut flush.

Published Sept. 1929. (250)

Contents:

p. 5–15   Text, dealing with the early poetry, the Nō plays, fiction, Ukiyo art, and literature.

Notes:

"The Monograph has been written for the British Group attending the Conference of the Institute of Pacific Relations at Kyoto in October 1929." p. [4]

Reprinted in *Pacific Affairs* (C30), and, in 1941, by the Society for International Cultural Relations (17a), with an added preface by the publishers. A brief description of the latter re-print is given because the rarity of the 1929 booklet might cause it to be overlooked.

A.W. included a translation, by Beryl de Zoete, of an eighth century Japanese ballad entitled "The Fisher-Boy of Urashima."

A17a THE ORIGINALITY / OF / JAPANESE CIVILIZATION / BY / ARTHUR WALEY / *K.B.S. 2600 Anniversary* / *Essay Series* / TOKYO / KOKUSAI BUNKA SHINKOKAI / [The Society for International Cultural Relations] / 1941

19 p.   21½ cm.

Boards covered with white paper printed with blue lozenge design. Blue label on front cover reads, within a double rule: THE ORIGINALITY / OF / JAPANESE CIVILIZATION / BY / ARTHUR WALEY White label on spine reads: THE ORGINALITY OF JAPANESE CIVILIZATION by A. WALEY

Published 1941 by Kokusai Bunka Shinkokai.

Contents:

The text is the same as that of A17. As the publisher's preface, p. 3–4, gives the impression that the booklet was specially written to commemorate the 2,600th anniversary of the foundation of the Japanese empire in 1940, it should be noted that Yukio Yashiro asked A.W., in a letter of April 16, 1940, for a contribution to celebrate the event. The result was the re-printing, in 1941, of the 1929 monograph.

A18 THE LADY / WHO LOVED INSECTS / TRANSLATED FROM THE / JAPANESE / BY / ARTHUR WALEY /DRY-POINTS BY HERMINE DAVID / London / The Blackamore Press / 1929

1l, 33 p. 2l, including front, and 3 other illus.   21½ cm.

"Printed in England at the Curwen Press," p. [8]

Bevelled boards covered with beige silk. On spine, in gold: THE / LADY / WHO / LOVED / INSECTS / [*at tail*] 1929. On front cover, in gold, vertically within a rectangle: THE LADY / WHO LOVED / INSECTS.   Top edge gilt, others untrimmed.

Published Dec. 1929 at 21/–. (550)

Contents:

	One blank leaf.
p. [2]	Statement of edition.
[3]	Half-title.
[6]	Frontispiece.
[7]	Title.

[9]   Engraved title.
11–33   Text.
[37]–[38]   Notes.
                 Three blank end-papers, the fourth being the
                 paste-down.

Notes:

Numbered edition. The first 50 copies were signed by A.W.,
printed on hand-made paper and covered in green silk.

The promised second chapter of the story does not exist. To
quote A.W.'s note on the piece: it ". . . is the third in the
collection of ten fragments known as the *Tsutsumi Chūnagon
Monogatari.* 'Tsutsumi Chūnagon,' 'The Counsellor of the Em-
bankment,' was Fujiwara no Kanesuke, who lived at the beginning
of the tenth century. But linguistic experts say that the stories
cannot be earlier than the twelfth. It is, however, by no means
certain that they are all by one hand or all date from the same
period."

The story was re-printed in *The Real Tripitaka* (A34).

A19   [*within an ornamental border, within a rule*] THE
BROADWAY TRAVELLERS / EDITED BY SIR
E. DENISON ROSS / AND EILEEN POWER /
[*printer's ornament*] / [*in red*] THE TRAVELS OF
/ AN ALCHEMIST / [*in black*] THE JOURNEY
OF THE TAOIST CH'ANG- / CH'UN FROM
CHINA TO THE HINDUKUSH / AT THE SUM-
MONS OF CHINGIZ KHAN / *Recorded by His
Disciple* / LI CHIH-CH'ANG / *Translated with an
Introduction by* / ARTHUR WALEY / [*rule*] / [*device

of sailing ship] / [*rule*] / *Published by* / [*in red*]
GEORGE ROUTLEDGE & SONS, LTD. / [*in black*]
BROADWAY HOUSE, CARTER LANE, LONDON
[1931]

8vo. xi, 166 p. 1l. front. [folding map]   22½ cm.

Printed by Headley Brothers, London and Ashford.

Red cloth boards, lettered in gold on spine: CH'ANG-
CH'UN / Travels of / an Alchemist / . / ARTHUR
WALEY / [*at tail*] [*ship device*] / ROUTLEDGE
All edges trimmed.

Published June 1931, at 10/6

Contents:

p.   vii–xi   Preface.
     1–40   Introduction.
               China and Central Asia at the time of
               Ch'ang-ch'un's journey. Chingiz and
               Mongol Religion, Chingiz and the Bud-
               dhists, Taoist indiscretions, Events after
               Ch'ang-ch'un's death.
     41–42   Sources.
     43–46   Sun Hsi's preface.
     47–157   Text.
     158–60   Appendix. [Information concerning the seven
               documents usually printed at the end of
               the *Hsi Yu Chi.*]
     161–66   Index.
               One leaf blank.

Notes:

"The *Hsi Yu Chi*, though its main interest is cultural and geographical, is also unique in its importance as a source for early Mongol history, enabling us as it does to fix with absolute certainty the otherwise obscure and much disputed dates of Chingiz Khan's movements during his Western campaign." (Preface, p. viii)

Impression:

Second, Aug. 1963.

A20 A CATALOGUE OF / PAINTINGS RE-COVERED / FROM TUN-HUANG BY / SIR AUREL STEIN, K.C.I.E. / PRESERVED IN THE SUB-DEPARTMENT / OF ORIENTAL PRINTS AND DRAWINGS / IN THE BRITISH MUSEUM, AND IN THE / MUSEUM OF CENTRAL ASIAN / ANTIQUITIES, DELHI / BY ARTHUR WALEY / *Formerly Assistant-Keeper in the / Sub-Department /* LONDON / PRINTED BY ORDER OF THE TRUSTEES / OF THE BRITISH MUSEUM AND OF THE / GOVERNMENT OF INDIA / 1931

4to. lii, 328 p.   26 cm.

Printed by John Johnson at the University Press, Oxford.

Black cloth boards, lettered on spine in gold: CATA-LOGUE OF / PAINTINGS / RECOVERED / FROM / TUN-HUANG / BY SIR / AUREL STEIN

/ WALEY / [*at tail*] 1931   Top and front edges trimmed.

Published Oct. 1931, at 40/–. (300?)

Contents:

p. [v]   Preface. Signed Laurence Binyon.
[ix]–lii   Introduction.
             The painters; style; iconography, (1) *Dhyāna; Meditation on Buddha*, (2) *Dhāranī and popular belief; Absence of Vairocana Buddhism; The anti-Buddhist measures of 841–5.* The Sadhanas. The paintings and the texts. The Amitābha-Amitāyus scriptures; *The Taima Mandara.* The paradise of Sākyamuni. Kshitigarbha. The world of the dead. Taoming and the golden-maned lion; *Mr. Justice Ts'ui.* Avalokiteśvara; *The eleven-faced Avalokiteśvara.* Tārā. Avalokiteśvara, by moonlit waters. Bhaishajyaguru. Maitreya. Manjusrī. The sūtras dealing with national safety. Vimalakīrti. The Arhats. The good boy and the bad boy. Apocryphal sūtras. Pigments. Costume; *The head dress of the donors; Dress of priests.* Rock temples; *The thousand Buddhas.* The mudrās.
1–211   Catalogue, Part I [with Addenda, p. 209–11]
213–314   Part II, Paintings in the Museum of Central Asian Antiquities, Delhi.

Notes:

The objects described were recovered by Sir Aurel Stein, during his expedition of 1906–8, from a walled-up chapel. Two fifths of the material went to the British Museum, and the remainder to the Museum of Central Asian Antiquities, Delhi. Dated works range between the years A.D. 846 and 943.

"As the most important of the paintings are re-produced in colour or monochrome in Sir Aurel Stein's *The Thousand Buddhas* (1921), no illustrations are given in this Catalogue." (Preface, p. [v])

A21 THE / LADY OF THE BOAT / BEING THE FIFTH PART OF / "THE TALE OF GENJI" / *by* / LADY MURASAKI / TRANSLATED FROM THE JAPANESE BY / ARTHUR WALEY / IN TWO VOLUMES / VOLUME ONE / LONDON / GEORGE ALLEN & UNWIN LTD / MUSEUM STREET [1932]

8vo. 309 p. 4l.   22 cm.

Printed by Unwin Brothers Ltd., Woking.

Grass-green cloth boards, blind stamped with a double line at head and tail on front board, lettered in gold on spine: [*double rule*] / THE LADY / OF THE / BOAT / By LADY / MURASAKI / [*leaf*] / ARTHUR /

WALEY / [*at tail*] GEORGE ALLEN / & UNWIN LTD / [*double rule*]   Edges trimmed head and tail.

Published June 1932, at 10/6. (1460 and 1040 for Houghton Mifflin)

Contents:

p. [9]	Preface.
15–309	Text. [Ch. I–Ch. VIII, 1st part]
2l	Advertisements.
2l	Blank.
	A third blank leaf [i.e., U8] was used as pastedown for cover.

Notes:

". . . It is Genji's reputed son . . . who is the hero of Volumes V and VI . . . . Between the end of Volume IV and the beginning of Volume V an interval of about eight years is evidently supposed to elapse, during which Genji dies." (Preface)

Some copies (of the first impression?) exist with the imprints of both publishers together on the title-page. There is on p. [29] of *The Bridge of Dreams* a list of *Errata* for *The Lady of the Boat.*

Impression:

Second, Feb. 1935, 450 copies and 500 for HM (printed in 1933).

Translation:

Turin, Bompiani, 1944.

A22   THE / BRIDGE OF DREAMS / BEING THE
SECOND VOLUME OF "THE LADY OF THE
BOAT" / AND THE FINAL PART OF "THE TALE
OF GENJI" / *by* / LADY MURASAKI / TRANS-
LATED FROM THE JAPANESE BY / ARTHUR
WALEY / LONDON / GEORGE ALLEN &
UNWIN LTD / MUSEUM STREET [1933]

8vo. 341 p. 1l.   22 cm.

Binding uniform with **A21**. Lettering uniform, except
title, which reads: THE BRIDGE / OF / DREAMS
Trimmed head and tail.

Published 2 May, 1933 at 10/6. (1650 and 1350 for
Houghton Mifflin)

Contents:

p. [11]–24   Introduction. Murasaki's affinities as a writer.
   [27]   Summary of the preceding volume.
   [29]   Errata in Volume V.
   32–341   Text. [Ch. VIII concluded–Ch. XIII]
[342]–[43]   Advertisements.

Notes:

Dedicated to W. Winkworth, p. [7].
A.W. prefers the first and last volumes of *Genji*, and, in the
introduction to this last volume, gives his reasons for finding it the
most successful of the six. The remarks on Murasaki's affinities
were prompted by the variety of authors to whom reviewers com-
pared her, ranging, in time, from Boccaccio to Proust.

In addition to the copies having the Allen and Unwin and the Houghton Mifflin imprints separately, some have title-pages bearing the two together.

Translation:

Turin, Bompiani, 1947.

A23 英 譯 中 國 歌 詩 選 / SELECT CHINESE VERSES / TRANSLATED BY / HERBERT A. GILES / AND / ARTHUR WALEY / THE COMMERCIAL PRESS, LIMITED / SHANGHAI, CHINA / 1934

1l. xi, 96 p. 1l.   19 cm.

Covers of grey paper impregnated with fine blue hairs.

Lettered on front cover: 英譯中國歌詩選   / SELECT CHINESE VERSES and on spine, bottom to top: SELECT   CHINESE   VERSES—GILES   AND WALEY on middle of back cover publisher's device, all printed in black. All edges trimmed flush with covers.

Published 1934 at 50 cents. (Shanghai)

Contents:

p.   [i]   Introduction, in Chinese, by Chang Yuan-
                    ch'i.
    [iii]   Publisher's Note.
    v–xi   List of Contents.
    [1]–46   Part I Translations by Herbert A. Giles.

47–96   Part II Translations by Arthur Waley.
[97]   Colophon in Chinese.

Notes:

The selections were made by Sir James Lockhart. A.W.'s work is represented by fifty-one pieces from 170 given here with the Chinese text. They are: Nos. 10, 13, 15 (2), 16, 17, 20–26, 28–30, 33, 35, 36, 38–41, 43, 44, 49–54, 59, 61, 63, 68, 70–72, 74, 85, 88–92, 95–97, 100, 101, 113 and 127.

A24   THE WAY AND ITS POWER / A *Study of the* / TAO TÊ CHING / *and* / *Its Place in Chinese Thought* / *by* / ARTHUR WALEY / LONDON / GEORGE ALLEN & UNWIN LTD / MUSEUM STREET [1934]

8vo. 262 p. 1l.   20½ cm.

Printed by Latimer Trend and Co., Plymouth.

Black cloth boards. Spine title, in gold, on pale blue blocked rectangle, reads: THE WAY / AND / ITS POWER / WALEY / [*at tail*] GEORGE ALLEN / & UNWIN LTD   Edges trimmed.

Published Oct. 1934, at 7/6. (1970)

Contents:

p.   11–15   Preface.
     17–100   Introduction.
              The Hedonists, Quietism, Taoism, The
              Language crisis, The Realists [Legalists],

Notes:

Dedicated to Leonard and Dorothy Elmhirst.

"But there exists no 'historical' translation [of the *Tao Tê Ching*]; that is to say, no attempt to discover what the book meant when it was first written. That is what I have tried to supply . . ." (Preface, p. 13)

"I want to make it clear that this translation of the *Tao Tê*

Ching is not literary; for the simple reason that the importance of the original lies not in its literary quality but in the things it says, and it has been my one aim to reproduce what the original says with detailed accuracy." (Preface, p. 14)

A.W. says also that he intends the book for those interested in the general history of mankind, for he finds that China has been relatively neglected in the general works.

The section entitled *The Language Crisis* (p. 59–68), dealing with the rift between language and actuality during the formative period of the Chinese language, was re-printed in *Polemic*, No. 4, July–August 1946, p. 5–9.

Impressions:

> Second, June 1937,   1000 copies.
> Third,   May 1942,   1250 copies.
> Fourth, June 1949,   2060 copies.
> Fifth,   Nov. 1956,   2000 copies.
> Grove Press, Jan. 1958, in the UNESCO collection of representative works—Chinese series, 7000 copies.

A25   THE BOOK OF / SONGS / *Translated from the* / *Chinese* / *by* / ARTHUR WALEY / LONDON / GEORGE ALLEN & UNWIN LTD / MUSEUM STREET [1937]

8vo. 358 p. 1l.   22½ cm.

Printed by Unwin Brothers Ltd., Woking.

Beige cloth boards, lettered on spine in gold: The Book / of Songs / ARTHUR WALEY / George Allen / and Unwin   Edges trimmed, top edge stained brown.

Published Sept. 1937, at 10/6. (1250 and 1250 for Houghton Mifflin)

Contents:

Notes:

Dedicated to Gustav Haloun.

A 32-page supplement containing textual notes was issued separately at the same time as the book.

Sixteen of the songs were first published in *Asia* (**B35**), and a group of political laments, omitted from the book, is discussed elsewhere (**C43**).

A.W. devotes p. 326 to a mention of the intrinsic quality of the *Songs*. He says that, since starting the study of them, in 1913, "the jumble of problems linguistic, botanic, zoological, historical, geographical which the translator of such a work must face, has never robbed the *Songs* of their freshness." For three early versions, see **A1**.

Benjamin Britten set two of the *Songs* to music from among those included in *Chinese Poems*, 1946 (**A30**).

Impressions:

Second (revised), Dec. 1954, 2050 copies. Produced by offset methods using as a basis corrected sheets of the first impression. The revision incorporated a new preface, some few textual changes (e.g., Song 20), and additional notes, thus superseding the first impression.

The revised text was used for an American impression published under the imprint of Grove Press, Feb. 1960, 7500 copies.

A26 *The Analects of / Confucius /* Translated and annotated / by / ARTHUR WALEY / London / GEORGE ALLEN & UNWIN LTD [1938]

8vo. 268 p. 2l.   22 cm.

Printed by Unwin Brothers Ltd., Woking.

Beige cloth boards, lettered on spine in black: *The / Analects / of / Confucius /* * / Arthur / Waley / * / George / Allen & / Unwin   Edges trimmed, top stained brown.

Published Nov. 1938, at 10/6. (2000)

Contents:

Notes:

Dedicated to C. G. Seligman.

Quotation beneath dedication reads: "True philosophy lies in being Humpty Dumpty without a great fall. May Chesshire."

"The present book is somewhat dry and technical in character. But I would not have it supposed that I have definitely abandoned literature for learning, or forgotten the claims of the ordinary reader. My next book, *Three Ways of Thought in Ancient China*, will be wholly devoid of technicalities and indeed in most ways a contrast to this work on the *Analects*." (Preface, p. 11)

Copies (of a trial binding-up?) exist cased in emerald-green cloth lettered in gold, and with top edge stained green.

Impressions:

Second, June 1945, 1,220 copies.
Third,   Aug. 1949, 2,127 copies.
Fourth, Dec. 1955, 2,525 copies.
Fifth,   1964.

Edition:

New York, Random House, April 1960, 15,000 copies, without the Textual Notes.

Translation:

Naarden (Holland), Toren, 1946.

A27   THREE WAYS / OF / THOUGHT / IN / ANCIENT / CHINA / by / Arthur / Waley / [*swelled rule*] / George Allen & Unwin Ltd / Museum Street, London [1939]

8vo. 275 p.   20 cm.

Printed by Unwin Brothers Ltd, Woking.

Beige cloth boards, lettered on spine in orange: THREE / WAYS / OF / THOUGHT / IN / ANCIENT / CHINA / [*hollow swelled rule*] / Arthur / Waley / [*at tail*] George Allen / & Unwin   Edges trimmed, top edge stained orange.

Published Nov. 1939, at 7/6. (2000)

Contents:

p.   11–14   Preface.
     17–112   Chuang Tzu.
              Part I. The realm of nothing whatever,
                 p. 17–86.
              Part II. Politics, p. 87–112.

Notes:

Dedicated to "The greatest traveller (See p. 61)." ["The greatest
traveller does not know where he is going; the greatest sight-seer
does not know what he is looking at," p. 61]

"This book consists chiefly of extracts from *Chuang Tzu, Mencius* and *Han Fei Tzu*." (Preface, p. 11)

Impressions:

Second, May 1947, 1750 copies.
Third, Mar. 1953, 2150 copies.
Fourth, Mar. 1964.

Editions:

New York, Doubleday, Mar. 1956, 25,000 copies, lacking the
Finding list and Textual notes.

Translations:

Hamburg, v. Schröder, 1947
Paris, Payot, 1949
There exists a Polish translation of p. 199–255 entitled *Realiści*,
32 p., bearing the imprint New York, 1957.

A28 [*in red upon decorations in grey*] TRANSLA-
TIONS / FROM THE / CHINESE / *by Arthur
Waley* / ILLUSTRATED BY / CYRUS LEROY
BALDRIDGE / *New York: Alfred A. Knopf: Mcmxli*

1l. [18], 325 p. 3l.   illus.   9 col. pl.   27½ cm.

"The Composition, Electrotyping, Printing and Binding were by The Haddon Craftsmen, Camden, New
Jersey." (Colophon p. [327])

Orange cloth-covered boards stamped in front, in black,
with design of a sage riding on a crane. On spine black
inked panel lettered in gold: [*between two rows of
printer's flowers and two dotted lines*] Translations /
from the / CHINESE / by / Arthur Waley / [*dotted
line*] / ILLUSTRATED BY / C. LEROY BALD-
RIDGE / [*dotted line*] / Alfred A. Knopf

Published Feb. 1941, at $5.00. (5000)

Contents:

p. [5]–[7]   Preface.
      3–325   Text.
     [327]   Colophon followed by two blank leaves.

Notes:

Apart from the Preface, Nos. 17, 69, 80, 133 and 134, the whole of 170 (**A2**) is collected in *Translations*. Except for one poem—No. 57—the volume also includes the complete *More Translations* (**A3**). There are no translations which are not in the two earlier books. *Chinese Poems* (**A30**) contains everything in *Translations*, and must be considered, in the absence of further revisions, to give A.W.'s preferred versions, although he mentions in his Preface that he has corrected a certain number of mistakes in the poems, as they stood in 1918 and 1919, for *Translations*. The second edition of 170, 1962, contains a few further corrections.

Impressions:

Second, Feb. 1945, 800 copies.
Third, Dec. 1945, 4875 copies.
Fourth, Mar. 1964, 3800 (approx.) copies.
At the time of first publication the Book-of-the-Month Club distributed an undisclosed number of additional copies to members.

A29 [*printed in brown upon a page decorated with a representation of a tortoise enlaced by a serpent*] MONKEY / *by* / Wu Ch'êng-ên / *Translated from the Chinese* / *by* / Arthur Waley / *London* / George Allen & Unwin Ltd [1942]

8vo. 305 p. 1l. 22 cm.

Printed by Unwin Brothers Limited, Woking.

Orange cloth boards, lettered on front board vertically downwards in green MONKEY 猴 and on spine horizontally / MONKEY / Wu / Ch'êng-ên / *trans-*

lated by / Arthur / Waley / [*at tail*] GEORGE ALLEN / AND UNWIN LTD Trimmed head and tail, top edge stained orange.

Published July 1942, at 12/6. (2750)

Contents:

p. 9–10 Preface.
11–305 Text.
One leaf blank.

Notes:

Dedication: To Beryl and Harold, p. [5]. (Beryl de Zoete and Harold Acton)

A.W. in his preface, says that he has reduced the number of episodes in this translation of the *Hsi Yu Chi*, but that those which he has retained have been translated almost in full "leaving out, however, most of the incidental passages in verse, which go very badly into English." (p. 9) The American edition contained a special introduction by Hu Shih, who gave therein detailed information concerning the parts omitted by A.W. and, on p. 306, recorded some points upon which he and A.W. differed.

For an original addition to the story, see **D9**.

The title-page and jacket of the English edition were designed by Duncan Grant.

Impressions:

Second, Feb. 1943, 2200 copies.
Third, July 1943, 2000 copies.
Fourth, Feb. 1944, 2900 copies.
Fifth, July 1946, 2900 copies.
Sixth, Aug. 1953, 2300 copies.
Seventh, 1965.

Editions:

New York, John Day, 1943. Another impression, Grove Press, July 1958, 8000 copies.
New York, John Day, 1944. (Adaptation for children)
London, Readers' Union, 1944.
Harmondsworth, England, Penguin Books, August 1961.

Translations:

Barcelona, Cervantes, 1945.
Zurich, Artemis, 1947.
Stockholm, Ljus, 1949.
Antwerp, Contact, 1950.
Paris, Payot, 1951.
Turin, Einaudi, 1960.
Matara [?], Ceylon, Saman Mudhnāly, 1962.

A30 ARTHUR WALEY / CHINESE POEMS / selected from / 170 CHINESE POEMS, MORE TRANSLATIONS / FROM THE CHINESE, THE TEMPLE / AND THE BOOK OF SONGS / [*Chinese motif printed in green*] / LONDON / GEORGE ALLEN AND UNWIN LTD [1946]

8vo. 213 p. 1l.   20½ cm.

Printed by Unwin Brothers Limited, London and Woking.

Emerald-green cloth boards, lettered on spine in gold: [*scroll*] / CHINESE / POEMS / *Arthur* / *Waley* / [*scroll*] / [*at tail*] *George Allen* / & *Unwin Ltd* Edges trimmed, top edge stained green.

Published Dec. 1946, at 8/6. (5000)

Contents:

Notes:

Dedicated to Edith Sitwell, p. [4].

In his preface A.W. refers to the fact that most of the poems in the book come from his earlier volumes and says that all the translations have been revised. The separate edition, with the Chinese text opposite the poems, which A.W. says he hopes to make, has not, as yet, appeared.

Chinese Poems contains twenty-eight poems from *The Book of Songs* (A25) (Nos. 238, 1, 2, 17, 20, 22–24, 26, 30–32, 36, 42, 56–58, 96, 116, 130, 131, 145, 160, 225, 274, 279, 286 and 206—but see second ed. of A25, 1954), all the translations in 170 except Nos. 2, 3, 5, 26, 29, 55, 56, 58 (1) and (2), 62, 64, 65, 70, 72, 78, 82, 96–98, 103–107 and 131. Of *More Translations* everything was included except Nos. 2, 3–5, 7, 10, 33, 60, 63, 65 and 68. All of the poems in the body of *The Temple* were included (except Nos. 1, 2, 9 and 16 as well as Li Hou-chu's "Immeasurable Pain" from Appendix I. Thus, all of *Translations* (A28) is here.

New material in *Chinese Poems*: Nos. (3), (4) and (5) of "Folk Songs," p. 108–9; Po Chü-i's "The Half-recluse" (B36), p. 179–80; and the anonymous "The Lady and the Magpie," p. 193.

"The Liberator" attributed to Wu-ti in 170 is given here to Ts'ao Chih; and "Summer Song," now assigned to Wu-ti, appeared as a "Tzǔ-yeh Song" in 170. "Dreaming of a dead lady" is now labelled Shên Yo, and "Song of the Snow-white heads," in 170 given to Cho Wēn-chün, has an anonymous attribution in *Chinese Poems*.

References are given after the title of each poem in the list of contents to facilitate consulting the Chinese originals.

Impressions:

Second, June 1948, 5000 copies.
Readers' Union (Book Club), 1949, 7270 copies.
Third, Dec. 1956, 2880 copies.
Fourth, 1962.

Edition:

Second, April 1961, omits the text references in the contents list, the additional notes, the index of first lines and authors' names, but includes a series of poems by Han-shan (**B43**) and one piece by Fēng Mēng-lung (**B45**). In a brief preface (dated May 1960) A.W. mentions changes made—and not made—for this edition. Another impression, 1964.

Translation:

Hamburg, v. Schröder, 1951.

Settings to music:

Pieces from *Chinese Poems* set to music are referred to by their numbering in the book in which they first appeared.

Robin Orr set **A2**, 60, 77, and 87 to music for voice and piano in *Three Chinese Songs*, 1947.

Peter Tranchell set **A2**, 95, **A3**, 16, 23, 26, 27, 35, 57 to music for baritone solo, string quartet and piano in *Seven Poems of Po Chü-i*, 1948. Also **A2**, 53 and 54 for baritone and small orchestra in *Two Poems of T'ao Ch'ien*, 1948.

Arthur Oldham set **A2**, 36 and 83 to music for high voice and piano in *Five Chinese lyrics*, 1951.

Benjamin Britten set **A2**, 18, 85, 99, **A3**, 27 (ii) and **A25**, 206, 286 to music for high voice and guitar in *Songs from the Chinese*, 1959.

A30a [*in brown calligraphic script*] IN THE GAL-LERY / by / ARTHUR WALEY / [*maze device*] / ILLUSTRATED BY / GEORGETTE BONER / 1949

30 p. 1l. Sewn in fours, with two blank paste-down leaves inserted at either end.   24 cm.

Printed in Zurich, Switzerland.

White paper covers bearing on front a green paper rectangle imprinted with a maze device in black. All edges cut flush.

Privately published by Miss Boner, 1949. (400 approx.)

Contents:

		One blank leaf.
p.	[3]	Title.
	5–30	Text.

Notes:

The text of the parable (the manuscript of which is owned by Miss Boner) was transcribed calligraphically and embellished with nineteen of the artist's line drawings. The work was then re-produced by an offset process, in brown ink throughout, on heavy wove paper. The story became more widely known when it was published in *The Cornhill* (**D11**). In 1964 it was included as one of the pieces in *The Secret History of the Mongols* . . . (**A40**).

Miss Boner translated *Monkey* (A29) into German, with Maria Nils, and for that edition executed 76 illustrations, some of which were used in the Dutch version.

A31   ARTHUR WALEY / THE LIFE AND TIMES / OF / PO CHÜ-I / 772–846 / A.D. / *LONDON* / GEORGE ALLEN & UNWIN LTD / RUSKIN HOUSE MUSEUM STREET [1949]

8vo. 238 p. 1l. front. port. map.   24 cm.

Printed by Unwin Brothers Ltd., London and Woking.

Light blue cloth boards, lettered on spine in gold: THE LIFE / AND / TIMES / OF / PO / CHÜ-I / [*rule*] / ARTHUR / WALEY / [*at tail*] ALLEN / AND / UNWIN   and, on top right-hand corner of front board, vertically downwards: 白樂天 Edges trimmed, top edge blue.

Published Dec. 1949 at 18/–. (3000)

Contents:

238   The Po family [*genealogical tree*].
              Folding map of China.
              One leaf blank.

Notes:

"My book is simply a history; I have invented neither incidents
nor thoughts . . ." A.W. goes on to mention matters which he
has deliberately avoided or treated summarily: Po's metrical technique and its relation to that of the poets who preceded and came
after him, his reputation as a writer, his relation to Buddhism and
political happenings during his lifetime. Poems which A.W. has
translated before (C30), he has tried not to repeat except where nec-
essary.
    Chapter I of the book first appeared in *The Cornhill Magazine*
(C53), a part of it, in German, in *Neue Auslese* (C56b), and part
of Chapter XI in *Ballet* (C56a), before publication.

Impressions:

Second, July 1957, 2000 copies.

Translation:

Tokyo, Misuzu Shoten, 1960.

A32 THE GREAT / SUMMONS / *By* CH'U
YUAN / [*calligraphic flourish*] / The WHITE
KNIGHT PRESS / HONOLULU, HAWAII · 1949

1l, 12 p. 1l.   23 cm.

Printed by A. Grove Day.

Stitched into pale green paper covers. Front cover lettered vertically in fancy script: CH'U YUAN and horizontally in bold: The Great Summons   Printed upon brown laid paper.

Distributed by Mr. and Mrs. Gregg M. Sinclair to their friends at Christmas.

Contents:

		One blank leaf.
p.	[1]	Title.
	3	Introduction by Mr. and Mrs. Sinclair.
	5–12	Text.
	[13]	Device of the White Knight Press in red.

Notes:

One hundred copies printed, p. [13]. Authorised by A.W., p. [2]. Originally printed in *More Translations*. The text of this edition is taken from a revised version in *Chinese Poems*, 1946.

A33   THE POETRY AND / CAREER OF / LI PO / 701–762 A.D. / By / ARTHUR WALEY / LONDON: GEORGE ALLEN AND UNWIN LTD / NEW YORK: THE MACMILLAN COMPANY [1950]

x, [2], 123 p.   19 cm.

Printed by Brown Knight & Truscott, Ltd., London.

Maroon cloth boards, lettered on spine in blue: THE / POETRY / AND / CAREER / OF / LI PO / — / ARTHUR / WALEY / [*at tail*] ALLEN / AND / UNWIN   Edges trimmed.

Published June 1951 at 8/6. (4000)

Contents:

Notes:

Number 3 in the series *Ethical and Religious Classics of East and West*.

". . . and here for the first time is a detailed account of Chinese society during a period of the Tang Dynasty, fertile in great poets . . ." (Note by the general editors, p. x).

No mention is made of the author's earlier *The Poet Li Po* (**A4**), either by editors or author.

Impressions:

Second, Aug. 1958, 2100 copies.

A34 THE REAL / TRIPITAKA / AND OTHER PIECES / [*solid swelled rule*] / ARTHUR WALEY

/ *LONDON* / GEORGE ALLEN AND UNWIN LTD / RUSKIN HOUSE MUSEUM STREET [1952]

8vo. 291 p.   22 cm.

Printed by Unwin Brothers Ltd, Woking and London.

Grey cloth-covered boards. Lettered on spine in green: THE / REAL / TRIPITAKA / [*swelled rule*] / ARTHUR / WALEY / [*at tail*] ALLEN & / UNWIN Edges trimmed, top edge stained green.

Published Feb. 1952 at 18/–. (4000)

Contents:

p.		
9–130	Part One. The Real Tripitaka.	
131–68	Part Two. Ennin and Ensai.	

Buddhism after Tripitaka's death. The Avatamsaka School. The T'ien-t'ai School. The rise of the Zen Sect. Tantric Buddhism and the Wu-t'ai Shan. Ennin's pilgrimage. Li Tê-yü. Taoism in Japan. Life at Yang-chow. The Embassy received at Ch'ang-an. Monk-tramps. The persecution. Opposition to the measures. Ensai.

169–213	Part Three. Eight Chinese Stories.	
	Tuan Ch'êng-shih	The King of Persia's Daughter. (**B37a, C50**)
		The Two Lunatics. (**B37a**)
	Lu Tzu	The old Nurse's Story. (**B37a**)

The notations in bold face following the individual pieces refer to the numbers of the entries in the bibliography which indicate the first appearance of a piece.

Notes:

Dedicated to Anna Boner, p. [6].
"I have merely tried to give the general reader a brief outline of the historical (as opposed to the legendary) Tripitaka's career" (Chapter I).

A35 *The Nine / Songs /* A STUDY OF SHAMAN-
ISM / IN ANCIENT CHINA / [*hollow swelled rule*]
/ ARTHUR WALEY / *LONDON* / GEORGE
ALLEN AND UNWIN LTD / RUSKIN HOUSE
MUSEUM STREET [1955]

8vo. 64 p.   22 cm.

Printed by Unwin Brothers Limited, Woking and London.

Pale blue cloth boards. Front board lettered: *The Nine
/ Songs / [hollow swelled rule]*. Spine lettered: *The /
Nine / Songs / [hollow swelled rule] / Arthur / Waley
/ [at tail] George / Allen / & / Unwin*

Published Feb. 1955, at 10/–. (1625)

Contents:

Notes:

Translation, with commentary, of the *Chiu Ko* section of *Ch'u Tz'u*, which A.W. touches on in *The Temple* (A10), p. 18 ff. The tenth song (No. 1 of 170) is given in *Chinese Poems*, 1946.

A.W. says that the book will be of interest chiefly to students of religion, though he adds: "But the Nine Songs are also well worth reading simply as poetry, and I have tried, within the limits of a literal translation, to make them sing as well as merely say." (Preface, p. [5])

"About the authorship of the Songs (that is to say, about the identity of the person who gave them their present form) and about their relations to the other pieces in the Ch'u Elegies I have deliberately said nothing." (Introduction, p. 17)

David Hawkes, in his *Ch'u Tz'ŭ*, Oxford, 1959, investigates the problem of the authorship of the Songs, acknowledges the help and encouragement of A.W. in his edition of the anthology and concludes tentatively that the ". . . author was a Ch'u poet writing not long after Ch'ü Yüan and familiar with his work."

Impressions:

Second, Sept. 1956, 2000 copies.

Translation:

Hamburg, v. Schröder, 1957.

A36 ALBERTO DE LACERDA / *77 Poems* / WITH A PREFACE BY / ARTHUR WALEY / TRANSLATED BY / ALBERTO DE LACERDA / AND / ARTHUR WALEY / GEORGE ALLEN &

UNWIN LTD / RUSKIN HOUSE MUSEUM STREET / LONDON [1955]

8vo. 85 p. 1l.   20 cm.

Printed by Robert MacLehose and Co. Ltd., The University Press, Glasgow.

Buff-yellow cloth boards, lettered in red on spine: *Alberto / de / Lacerda / 77 / Poems / George / Allen / & / Unwin*   Edges trimmed.

Published May 1955, at 9/6. (2000)

Contents:

p.   7–8   Preface (Signed Arthur Waley).
    12–85   Text of poems.
             One leaf of advertisements.

Notes:

Dedication, p. [5], reads: *Para a Sophia.*
Portuguese and English text on facing pages.
On p. [6] two quotations which read as follows:

Le but de la vie, c'est de construire une architecture dans l'âme
                    SIMONE WEIL

a alegria é a coisa mais séria da vida
joy is the most serious thing in life
    ALMADA NEGREIROS

The Preface consists of a note on Alberto de Lacerda's poetical work together with an explanation of how the translations were made. A.W. later dedicated *Ballads and stories* . . . (A39) to the poet.

A37 ARTHUR WALEY / YUAN MEI / *Eighteenth Century* / *Chinese Poet* / Il est probable qu'il n'y a rien de plus / sain pour un homme, comme pour / tout animal, que de suivre ses goûts. / *Remi de Gourmont* / *LONDON* / GEORGE ALLEN AND UNWIN LTD / Ruskin House Museum Street [1956]

8vo. 227 p. front. port.   22½ cm.

Printed by Unwin Brothers Limited, Woking and London.

Black cloth boards, lettered on spine in silver: AR-THUR / WALEY / YUAN / MEI / [*flower*] / [*at tail*] GEORGE / ALLEN / AND / UNWIN   Edges trimmed, top edge stained green.

Published Jan. 1957 at 21/–. (3000)

Contents:

Notes:

Dedicated to Osbert Sitwell.

Appendix I, Yuan Mei's account of Anson's visit to Canton in 1743, first appeared in *History Today*, April 1956 (**C70**).

A.W., in his preface, says: "There is still scope for a full-scale biography, addressed to specialists, and dealing with every aspect of his life and writings. I have concentrated rather on whatever in his story has a general human interest, and on translating such of his poems as can be made intelligible without an undue amount of explanation."

Impressions:

Second, June 1958, 2000 copies.

Grove Press, Aug. 1958, 5000 copies.

A38 ARTHUR WALEY / [*swelled rule*] / *The Opium War* / *Through* / *Chinese Eyes* /*Ruskin House* / GEORGE ALLEN & UNWIN LTD / MUSEUM STREET LONDON [1958]

8vo. 257 p. 1l.   22 cm.

Printed by Unwin Brothers Ltd, Woking and London.

Brown simulated cloth boards. Lettered on spine in aluminium: ARTHUR / WALEY / [*swelled rule*] /

The / *Opium* / *War* / *Through* / *Chinese* / *Eyes*
/ [*at tail*] George / Allen / & / Unwin   Edges
trimmed, top edge stained brown.

Published Nov. 1958, at 21/–. (3120)

Contents:

p.   7–8   Preface.
     11–244   Text, divided into five parts: I. *Commissioner
               Lin at Canton.* II. *Songs of Oh dear, Oh
               dear!* III. *Shanghai.* IV. *Chinkiang.* V.
               Gutzlaff and his traitors. Mamo.
     245   Appendix. *Palmerston's letter to the 'Min-
               ister of the Chinese Emperor.'*
     246–47   Dates. [1839–42]
     248   Chinese sources.
     249–57   Index.
   [259]–[60] Advertisements.

Notes:

A.W. bases his account of what the war felt like on the Chinese
side largely on Chinese sources and principally on the *Ya-p'ien
Chan-cheng Tzu-liao Ts'ung-k'an*, 6 vols., Shanghai, 1955, which
printed many of Commissioner Lin's papers for the Opium War
period. The title of Part II comes from another Chinese book,
the *Tu-tu yin* of Pei Ch'ing-ch'iao. As elsewhere, A.W. says that
he writes chiefly for the general reader.

Impression:

Second, 1965?

· 89 ·

A39 ARTHUR WALEY / BALLADS AND / STORIES / FROM / TUN-HUANG / AN AN-THOLOGY / *Ruskin House* / GEORGE ALLEN & UNWIN LTD / MUSEUM STREET LONDON [1960]

8 vo. 273 p. 1l.   22 cm.

Printed by Unwin Brothers Ltd, Woking and London.

Dark blue simulated cloth boards. Lettered on spine in aluminium: ARTHUR / WALEY / [*hollow swelled rule*] / BALLADS / AND / STORIES / FROM / TUN- / HUANG / [*at tail*] GEORGE / ALLEN / AND / UNWIN   Edges trimmed, top edge stained blue.

Published Nov. 1960, at 25/–. (3420)

Contents:

(2) *Text about the arrest of Chi Pu, in one chapter.*

(3) *The story of Wang Chao-chün.*

IV. "Aucassin et Nicolette."

V. List of dates.

Notes:

Dedicated to Alberto de Lacerda.

Translations, in whole or part, of 26 of the 78 pieces of popular literature included in the *Tun-huang Pien-wên Chi,* 1957.

One of the pieces, *T'ien K'un-lun,* had been previously published by A.W. (**B44**)

He points out that his collection is intended for the general reader and devotes another article (**C76**) to certain linguistic problems not included in the Notes and References. For A.W.'s other writings relating to Tun-huang, see the Index.

A40   ARTHUR WALEY / THE SECRET / HISTORY OF / THE MONGOLS / AND OTHER PIECES / *London* / GEORGE ALLEN & UNWIN LTD / RUSKIN HOUSE   MUSEUM STREET [1964]

8vo. 320 p.   22 cm.

Printed by Unwin Brothers Limited, Woking and London.

Crimson simulated cloth boards. Lettered in aluminium
on spine, on a blue background within an aluminium
box: ARTHUR / WALEY / [*rule*] / THE / SECRET
/ HISTORY / OF THE / MONGOLS / [*at tail*]
GEORGE / ALLEN / AND / UNWIN   Edges
trimmed, top edge stained blue.

Published Jan. 1964 at 32/–.

Contents:

211–13	The owl speaks. An Ainu story.	(B36a)
217–91	The Secret History of the Mongols.	
292–93	La Vie de Pierre Ruffin, a review.	
294–96	The Coal-scuttle.	
297–302	The Hymn of the soul.	(B42)
	Original pieces.	
305–8	The Presentation.	(D4)
309–16	In the Gallery.	(A30a)
316	Censorship.	(D6)
317–18	No Discharge.	(D7)
319	Blitz poem.	
	Song.	
320	The Swan.	(D7a)

The notations in bold face following each piece refer to the number of the entry in the bibliography which indicates the first appearance of that piece.

Notes:

A.W. says in his preface that he regards the historical value of the *Secret History* as almost nil, that it is its quality as primitive literature which interests him and that he has translated only the parts founded on story-tellers' tales. For comments on some textual matters in the Chinese version, which A.W. used here, see C77.

Of the other pieces printed here for the first time, that on Blake was broadcast by the BBC in January 1948, "The Coal-scuttle" is a translation of Kafka's "Der Kübelreiter," and "Blitz Poem" and "Song" are original poems. The review appeared in the *Times Literary Supplement*, July 24, 1930, p. 612 (see note preceding Section E).

B: FIRST APPEARANCES OF TRANSLATIONS

This list records translations which were first published in periodicals. It does not include re-printings in
other periodicals from these original appearances, nor
does it list re-printings of translations after they had
once been collected into a book.

Some of the periodicals, all published in the United
States, which re-printed A.W.'s work in either of the
two ways mentioned are listed below. Dates between
which most interest was expressed follow the titles.

> *Living Age,* 1918–19.
> *Survey,* 1919.
> *Literary Digest,* 1919–26.
> *Independent and Weekly Review,* 1921.
> *Golden Book,* 1925–28.
> *Woman's Home Companion,* 1944.

B1 "Pre-T'ang Poetry" in *Bulletin of the School of
Oriental Studies,* [Vol. I, Pt. I], 1917, p. 34–52.

All the thirty-seven poems were re-printed in A *hundred and
seventy Chinese Poems* (A2, *q.v.*). At that time none of them had
been translated before.

B2 "Thirty-eight poems by Po Chü-i" in *Bulletin of
the School of Oriental Studies,* [Vol. I, Pt. I], 1917, p.
53–78.

All of the translations were re-printed in *170* (A2, *q.v.*).

A.W., in his introduction, notes that only three of them had
been previously translated (Nos. 8, 11 and 14). He adds a "Note
on the metre of the Translations" saying: "I have therefore tried

to produce regular rhythmic effects similar to those of the original. Each character in the Chinese is represented by a stress in the English . . ."

B3 "Poems of Po Chü-i" in *The Little Review*, Vol. IV, No. 6, Oct. 1917, p. 3–7.

Eight poems, all re-printed in 170 (**A2**, *q.v.*). The poem here entitled "Immortality" is re-named "Magic" in the book.

B4 "Poems by Po Chü-i" in *The New Statesman*, Oct. 13, 1917, p. 37–38.

Seven poems, all re-printed in 170 (**A2**, *q.v.*). A.W. adds a short note (7 lines) on the poet's satire, which follows "The Old Man with the Broken Arm."

B5 "Poems by Po Chü-i" in *The New Statesman*, Nov. 24, 1917, p. 185–86.

Ten poems, all re-printed in 170 (**A2**, *q.v.*). An untitled poem is called "Ease" in the book.

B6 "Poems of Po Chü-i" in *The Little Review*, Vol. IV, No. 8, Dec. 1917, p. 23–27.

"I reprint these poems from the October number. They are too good for anyone to miss. M.C.A"[nderson].

B7 "Further poems by Po Chü-i, and an extract from his prose works, together with two other T'ang poems" in *Bulletin of the School of Oriental Studies*, [Vol. I, Pt. 2], 1918, p. 96–112.

Of the twenty-two further poems, all except No. 13, "The Little Nun at Lung Hua Monastery," were re-printed in *More Translations* (**A3**, *q.v.*). The prose work is entitled "Record of a strange

Experience." A poem by Li Po, A.W. translates as "Ballad of Lü Water," giving translations by Judith Gautier in French and by Anna von Bernhardi in German. A hitherto untranslated poem by Tu Fu, A.W. translates as "A Song of Kao Hsien-chih's Blue Colt," adding in his introduction: "These will enable the reader to estimate the immense originality of Po Chü-i, who almost alone of T'ang poets, avoided the pedantry of obscure literary allusion."

B8 "Chinese Poems" in *Poetry*, Vol. XI, No. IV, Jan. 1918, p. 198–200.

Seven poems, two of which were not apparently re-printed: T'ang Seng-ch'i's "On finding a hairpin in a disused well" and "On seeing swallows in his prison cell" by Wang Tzu-tuan. The others were all re-printed in *170* (**A2**, *q.v.*), where the poem "In a jade Cup" becomes "Businessmen" and "What should a man want" is entitled "Tell me now."

B9 "Chinese Poems" in *Poetry*, Vol. XI, No. V, Feb. 1918, p. 252–54.

Three poems, all re-printed in *170* (**A2**, *q.v.*). "On barbarous modern Instruments" is re-named "The Old Harp" in the book and "The Old Lute" in *Chinese Poems*, 1946.

B10 "Chinese Poems" in *The New Statesman*, Feb. 2, 1918, p. 426–27.

Eight poems, all re-printed in *170* (**A2**, *q.v.*).

B11 "Hearing that his Friend was coming back from the War" in *The Nation*, May 4, 1918, p. 115. (Wang Chien)

Re-printed in *More Translations* (**A3**).

B12 "Chinese Poems" in *The New Statesman*, May 18, 1918, p. 131–32.

Nine poems, all re-printed in *170* (**A2**, *q.v.*).

B13 "Crossing an Old Battlefield at Night" in *The Nation*, Aug. 17, 1918, p. 526. (Tou Hsiang)

Apparently not re-printed.

B13a "To the bachelor-of-arts P'ei Ti" in *Reconstruction* (Society of Friends), Vol. I, No. 9, Dec. 1918, p. 150–51. (Wang Wei)

Re-printed in *More Translations* (**A3**).

B14 "The Great Summons" in *The New Statesman*, May 31, 1919, p. 215–16. (Ch'ü Yüan)

Re-printed in *More Translations* (**A3**).

B15 "The Story of Ts'ui Ying-ying, by Yüan Chēn" in *The English Review*, Vol. XXIX, July 1919, p. 32–41.

Re-printed in *More Translations* (**A3**).

B16 "The Pitcher" in *The New Statesman*, July 5, 1919, p. 347. (Yüan Chēn)

Re-printed in *More Translations* (**A3**).

B17 "The Nō: a few translations" in *Transactions and Proceedings of the Japan Society*, Vol. XVII, 1918–20, p. 100–26.

As an introduction A.W. gives a version of *The Duchess of Malfi* as it might be treated in a Nō play. The translations were all re-printed in *The Nō plays* (**A6**, *q.v.*).

B17a "The Master of the Five Willows, an autobiography" in *The Borzoi 1920*, New York, 1920, p. 52. (T'ao Ch'ien)

Translated for A. A. Knopf's "sort of record of five years' publishing," which also contains (p. 24–27) an article by Joseph Hergesheimer entitled: "A note on the Chinese poems translated by Arthur Waley."

B18 "Buddha's Pity" in *The New Statesman*, Feb. 28, 1920, p. 616–17.

Re-printed in *The Temple* (**A10**).

B19 "Early Snow, a Nō play" in *Poetry*, Vol. XV, Mar. 1920, p. 317–20.

Re-printed in *The Nō plays* (**A6**).

B20 "Chorus from the Nō-play Hōkazō" in *The New Statesman*, Sept. 11, 1920, p. 621.

Re-printed in *The Nō Plays* (**A6**).

B21 "Some Poems from the Manyōshu and Ryōjin Hisshō" in *The Journal of the Royal Asiatic Society*, April 1921, p. 193–203.

Translations, with romaji text, of 36 poems from the *Manyō*: 95, 123, 124, 125, 142, 607, 1158, 1165, 1235, 1257, 1263, 1777, 1796, 1885, 1892, 1949, 2368, 2495, 2550, 2564, 2687, 2841, 2855, 2859, 2869, 3350, 3399, 3455, 3459, 3476, 3517, 3873, 4285, 4389, 4405, 4431 in the *Kokka Daikwan*, together with 14 previously untranslated folk-poems from the *Ryōjin Hisshō*, re-discovered in 1911. All 50 poems were re-printed in **G1** and in **A40**. Both re-printings retain the misnumbering in the article, where 3350 is wrongly numbered 3149 and 3399 is wrongly called 3350.

B22 "On the criticism, collection, purchase and handling of pictures" in *Asia Major*, Hirth Anniversary Volume, 1923, p. 417–20.

Translation from the *Li T'ai Ming Hua Chi* by Chang Yen-yüan, completed in 847. For further references to Chang, see *An Introduction* . . . , p. 161–62 (**A9**).

B23 "Poverty" in *The Spectator*, 13 Jan. 1923, p. 58. (Yang Hsiung)

Re-printed in *The Temple* (**A10**).

B24 "The Bones of Chuang Tzu" in *The London Mercury*, Feb. 1923, p. 348–50. (Chang Hēng)

Re-printed in *The Temple* (**A10**).

B25 "The Cicada" in *Asia*, April 1923, p. 262. (Ou-yang Hsiu)

Re-printed in *The Temple* (**A10**).

B26 "The Nightmare" and "Hot cakes" in *The Chapbook*, No. 38, June 1923, p. 12–14. (Wang Yen-shou and Shu Hsi)

Re-printed in *The Temple* (**A10**).

B27 "Three poems by the priest Chiao-Jan (About 730–800 A.D.)" in *The Spectator*, Oct. 13, 1923, p. 500.

"The little waterfall," "Summer evening" and "Late snow." Not apparently re-printed elsewhere.

B28 "A Chinaman's description of Brighton in 1877" in *The New Statesman*, Dec. 15, 1923, p. 302–3.

Written by Li Shu-ch'ang, who was secretary to the first Chinese ambassador to Great Britain. Re-printed at the end of Chapter XIX of *Brighton*, by Osbert Sitwell and Margaret Barton, London, 1935.

B29 "Early Japanese folk-song (8th century A.D.)" in *The Spectator*, Jan. 19, 1924, p. 87.

Not apparently re-printed elsewhere.

B30 "Clouds by Night" in *The Nation*, July 11, 1925, p. 460. (Kuo Ch'en)

Not apparently re-printed elsewhere.

B31 "Foreign Fashions" in *The Forum*, July 1927, p. 3. (Po Chü-i)

Not apparently re-printed elsewhere.

B32 "Three Chinese Poems" in *The Forum*, June 1928, p. 877–80.

Han Yü.   The Banquet
Po Chü-i   Harp in the Garden
            The Mulberry Tree. Illustrated with block-prints by
            L. L. Balcom. Not apparently re-printed.

B33 "A modern Chinese essayist" in *The New Statesman*, Sept. 14, 1929, p. 679–80.

Translated from the Chinese of the contemporary humorist Ch'iu-lang.

B34 "Singing-girl" in *Asia,* Nov. 1929, p. 876–77, 904–7.

Extract from Liu T'ieh-yün's autobiographical novel *The Wanderings of Lau Ts'an,* 1906.

B35 "Courtship and Marriage in early Chinese Poetry" in *Asia,* June 1936, p. 403–6.

After a short explanatory introduction, A.W. gives two groups of translations from *The Book of Poetry* dealing respectively with courtship and marriage. The poems were later re-printed in *The Book of Songs* numbered as follows: 8, 22, 24, 28, 54, 32, 57, 62 and 75, 88, 93, 97, 98, 103, 106, 116.

B35a "Ainu Song" in *The Listener,* Oct. 26, 1939, p. 812.

Re-printed in **A40**.

B36 "The Half-recluse" in *The New Statesman,* Aug. 7, 1943, p. 88. (Po Chü-i)

Re-printed in **A30**.

B36a "Two Ainu Fables" in W. Sansom, *Choice,* London, 1946, p. 112–16.

"The Owl" was re-printed in *The New Statesman,* Sept. 11, 1948, p. 212, and, under another title, in **A40**. "The Little Wolf" does not seem to have appeared elsewhere. The stories come from *Ainu Shinyō Shū,* by Y. Chiri, Tokyo, 1926.

B36b "The Dancing Horses: translated from the *Ming Huang Tsa Lu* of Chêng Ch'u-hui (c. 850 A.D.)" in *Ballet,* Vol. 2, No. 1, June 1946, p. 62–63.

A story, re-printed in *The Real Tripitaka* (**A34**, *q.v.*).

B37 "Mrs. White" in *Horizon*, Vol. XIV, Aug. 1946, p. 86–112.

An anonymous eighteenth century story, re-printed in **A34**, and in *The Golden Horizon*, edited by Cyril Connolly, London, 1953, p. 259–85.

B37a "Three T'ang stories" in *Lilliput*, June 1947, p. 543–46.

All re-printed in *The Real Tripitaka* (**A34**, *q.v.*).

B38 "Three T'ang stories" in *The Cornhill Magazine*, Vol. 163, Spring 1948, p. 118–23.

All re-printed in *The Real Tripitaka* (**A34**, *q.v.*).

B39 "San Sebastian" in *Horizon*, Vol. XX, Sept. 1949, p. 190–200. (R. Akutagawa)

A.W. in a brief introduction to this piece, when it was re-printed in *The Real Tripitaka* (**A34**), calls it a scenario. Akutagawa's original title was *Yūwaku* ("Temptation"). It comes from the posthumous volume *Konan no Ōgi* ("The Honan Fan"), Tokyo, 1928.

B40 "Kitune Shirka: the Ainu epic" in *Botteghe Oscure*, Vol. VII, 1951, p. 214–36.

A.W. gives some information about the history of the poem, which was published only in 1932, in a short note which follows his translation. Re-printed in **A40**.

B41 "Recent Chinese Poetry" in *Arena*, Vol. II, No. 7, April/May 1951, p. 3–8.

Contains translations of "Shanghai" and "Shanghai Winter" by Ma Fan-to, "Song of Exile" by Ma Yin-yin, "Into Battle" and "The Sword" by I Men.

B42 "The Hymn of the Soul" in *Encounter*, Vol. I, No. 3, Dec. 1953, p. 26–28.

Translation of a non-Christian Gnostic hymn preserved in the apocryphal *Acts of Thomas*, which exists in a Greek and a Syriac version. A.W. used the Syriac text as well as W. Wright's translation: *The Apocryphal Acts of the Apostles*, 1871. Re-printed in **A40**.

B43 "27 Poems by Han-shan" in *Encounter* 12, Sept. 1954, p. 3–8.

A brief biographical note on the Recluse of the Cold Mountain precedes the text of the untitled Buddhist mystical poems, selected from just over three hundred which survive. Re-printed in *Chinese Poems*, second ed. (**A30**).

B44 "An early Chinese Swan-maiden story" in *Journal of the Warburg and Courtauld Institutes*, Vol. XXII, Nos. 1 and 2, Jan.–June 1959, p. 1–5.

A.W. dates the story, the MS of which came from Tun-huang, at about the ninth century A.D. He mentions a quasi-Swan-maiden story in the *Hsüan-chung Chi*, c. A.D. 300. Re-printed, with notes, in **A39**, p. 149–54. See also A. T. Hatto, "The Swan Maiden: a folk-tale of north Eurasian origin" in *BSOAS*, Vol. XXIV, 1961, p. 326–52.

B45 "Song" in *Evergreen Review*, Nov.–Dec. 1959, p. 47. (Fêng Mêng-lung)

Re-printed in *Chinese Poems*, 2d. ed. (**A30**).

B46 "A Song from Tun-huang" in *Bulletin of the School of Oriental Studies*, Vol. XXVI, 1963, p. 149–51.

Translation, with photograph, of the text of *Hsi ch'iu t'ien* from the back of No. 6714 of Giles's *Catalogue* . . .

C: ARTICLES

C1 "A Chinese picture" in *Burlington Magazine*, Jan. 1917, p. 3–10.

Discusses the British Museum's copy of Chang Tsē-tuan's painting, "Going up the River for the Spring Festival."

C2 "The rarity of Ancient Chinese paintings" in *Burlington Magazine*, June 1917, p. 209–14.

C3 "A Chinese portrait" in *Burlington Magazine*, Oct. 1917, p. 131.

A rubbing of an incised portrait of T'ung Wu, c. 1309.

C4 "Notes on Chinese prosody" in *Journal of the Royal Asiatic Society*, 1918, p. 249–61.

Deals with tone, rhyme, rhyme and tone-arrangement, cæsura, "new style" and "old style" poetry.

C5 "Recent acquisitions for public collections—VII" in *Burlington Magazine*, Feb. 1919, p. 55.

A sketch from Tun-huang for the Print Room of the British Museum.

C6 "Note on the invention of Woodcuts" in *The New China Review*, Vol. I, No. 4, Aug. 1919, p. 412–15.

A.W. re-examines the textual evidence in the *Ko-Chih Ching Yuan*, and concludes that the date of 593 generally accepted as the earliest literary reference to book printing from wood-blocks is not indubitable. He prefers Liu P'in's mention of c. 880, and suggests that the art travelled to China, with Buddhism, from the West. See T. F. Carter, *The Invention of Printing in China* . . . , New York, 1955, p. 40 and note 12.

C7 "The poet Li Po (A.D. 701–762)" in *The Asiatic Review*, Vol. XV, Oct. 1919, p. 584–610.

Also published separately. For contents, see **A4**.

C8 "A painting by Yen Li-pēn" in *Burlington Magazine*, Nov. 1919, p. 198.

Reproduction of part of a picture of thirteen famous emperors, supposedly by Yen Li-pēn.

C9 "Hymns to Kuan-yin" in *Bulletin of the School of Oriental Studies*, Vol. I, Pt. III, 1920, p. 145–46.

Translations of two hymns on a picture in the Stein Collection (B.M. 1919.1.1.104) dated A.D. 910.

C10 "Notes on the 'Lute-girl's song'" in *The New China Review*, Vol. II, 1920, p. 591–97.

A.W. supplies the preface of a poem by Po Chü-i, translated by Professor H. A. Giles (*Chinese Literature*, p. 165), thus explaining the circumstances under which it was written (see *The Life and Times* . . . , p. 117). He adds criticism of a few points in Giles's translation and replies to the latter's remarks (*NCR* Vol. II, 1920, p. 319–40) concerning the translation of "The Great Summons" in *More Translations*. Giles continues in *NCR* Vol. III, 1921, p. 281–88.

C11 "Chinese philosophy of Art" in *Burlington Magazine*, Dec. 1920, p. 309–10.

I. Note on the six "methods."
———Jan. 1921, p. 32.

II. Wang Wei and Chang Yen-yüan.
————Mar. 1921, p. 111–12.
III. Ching Hao.
————May 1921, p. 244.
IV. Kuo Hsi (Part I)
————July 1921, p. 10–11.
V. Kuo Hsi (Part II)
————Aug. 1921, p. 84.
VI.
————Sept. 1921, p. 128.
VII. Tung Ch'i-ch'ang (I)
————Nov. 1921, p. 235–36.
VIII.
————Dec. 1921, p. 292.
IX. (Concluded)

C12   "Leibniz and Fu Hsi" in *Bulletin of the School of Oriental Studies*, Vol. II, Pt. I, 1921, p. 165–67.

Fu Hsi's use of a binary notation known to Leibniz. For further discussion, see J. Needham, *Science and civilisation in China*, Vol. II, *History of Scientific Thought*, 1956, p. 340–45.

C13   "Two notes on Nō" in *Bulletin of the School of Oriental Studies*, Vol. II, Pt. I, 1921, p. 167–70.

"These notes are supplementary to . . . *The Nō plays of Japan*" [*q.v.*]. They deal with the dates of Kwanami and Seami, as well as the allusiveness of the Nō plays.

C14   "Yūgen" in *The New Statesman*, Mar. 26, 1921, p. 729.

Discusses "what lies beneath the surface" in Nō, and its value for Western drama. Contains some material not wholly in *The Nō Plays . . .* (A6).

C15 "Confucius" in *Form*, Vol. I, No. 1, Oct. 1921, p. 9–12.

Compares the ideas of Confucius with those of the twentieth century.

C16 "An introspective romance" in *The New Statesman*, Dec. 10, 1921, p. 286–87.

A.W. deals with the current preference for Chinese art over Japanese, speaks of Japanese literature and an episode from *Genji Monogatari*.

C17 "The Everlasting Wrong" in *Bulletin of the School of Oriental Studies*, Vol. II, Pt. II, 1922, p. 343–44.

Discusses differences in A.W.'s translation of Po Chü-i's poem and the version of Professor Giles.

C18 "Ricci and Tung Ch'i-ch'ang" in *Bulletin of the School of Oriental Studies*, Vol. II, Pt. II, 1922, p. 342–43.

Warns against attaching too great an importance to inscriptions on paintings. A.W. quotes a passage of Tung's own writings which shows that he studied Christianity.

C19 "Chinese temple paintings" in *Burlington Magazine*, Nov. 1922, p. 228.

Chang Yen-yüan's remarks on the principal works of art in the temples of Ch'ang-an and Lo-yang before the laïcization of A.D. 845.

C20 "T'ai Tsung's six chargers" in *Burlington Magazine*, Sept. 1923, p. 117–18.

Corrects an article in the *Museum Journal*, Philadelphia, concerned with the reliefs.

C21 "Avalokiteśvara and the legend of Miao-shan" in *Artibus Asiae*, No. 1, 1925, p. 130–32.

A.W. submits that there is no reason to think that the worship of a native Chinese mother-goddess favoured the sex-transformation of Avalokiteśvara.

C22 "Christ or Bodhisattva?" in *Artibus Asiae*, No. 1, 1925, p. 5.

Note on a fragmentary painting (illustrated) in the British Museum (Stein Collection No. 48).

C22a "The Gossamer Diary" in *The Calendar of Modern Letters*, Sept. 1925, p. 34–43.

Translation, with some commentary, of parts of the *Kagerō Nikki* written by the mistress of Fujiwara no Kane-iye (929–99). His legitimate son Michinaga courted Murasaki, the authoress of *The Tale of Genji*. A.W. says: "We find in the *Gossamer Diary* an anticipation of just those characteristics which mark off Genji from other Japanese romances . . ." Re-printed in A12. A translation of the whole work by Edward Seidensticker was published in Tokyo in 1964.

C23 "The Quartette" in *The New Statesman*, Jan. 1926, p. 356–57.

Discussion of the four component parts of Japanese fiction: narrative of events, dialogue, psychology and the comments of the author. The value of the classification for the Western writer.

C24 "The T'ao-t'ieh" in *Burlington Magazine*, Feb. 1926, p. 104.

Calls attention to Lu Pu-wei's explanation of the mask, from the *Lü-shih Ch'un Ch'iu*. The T'ao-t'ieh is, according to this, the symbol of an acquisitive state, itself on the verge of extinction.

C25 "Momoshiki no and Atago" in *Ostasiatische Zeitschrift*, Vol. 14, 1927, p. 157.

Note on the translation of two words used in the Genji translation to which a reviewer took exception.

C26 "Note on the names Kwanze, Kongō etc." in *Ostasiatische Zeitschrift*, Vol. 14, 1/2 Heft, 1927, p. 61.

A.W. gives the source for the connecting of the two Nō schools with Buddhism.

C27 "Shiba Kōkan (1737–1818)" in *Ostasiatische Zeitschrift*, Vol. 15, 2 Heft, 1927, p. 60–75.

Biographical sketch of "the first person in Japan to feel that to be Far Eastern meant, in the world sense, to be provincial. . . ." Note on Kōkan as an artist, list of nineteen of his paintings with one, of a Chinese beauty, reproduced. T. Muraoka's edition of Kōkan's *Tenchi-Ridan* (Tokyo, 1930) gives further information. Re-printed in **A40**.

C28 "Shiba Kōkan and Harushige not identical" in *Burlington Magazine*, April, 1928, p. 178.

Shows how Kōkan was not, and never claimed to be, Harushige.

C29 "Shiba Kōkan and Harushige identical" in *Burlington Magazine*, Aug. 1929, p. 73–74.

A.W.'s reply to K. Tomita's remarks concerning the preceding article.

C30 "The Originality of Japanese Civilization" in *Pacific Affairs*, No. 12, Dec. 1929, p. 767–73.

Separately published by the Oxford University Press; see **A17**.

C31 "Notes on Chinese alchemy (supplementary to Johnson's A *study of Chinese alchemy*)" in *Bulletin of the School of Oriental Studies*, Vol. VI, Pt. I, 1930, p. 1–24.

See also **C36**.

C32 "Downhill (Apropos of the Kandahar race at St. Anton, on March 15th.)" in *The Nation*, Mar. 29, 1930, p. 891.

A.W. writes of the "aesthetic" quality in ski-ing.

C33 "Magical use of phallic representations; its late survival in China and Japan" in *Bulletin of the Museum of Far Eastern Antiquities*, Stockholm, No. 3, 1931, p. 61–62.

Complementary notes to B. Karlgren's article, "Some fecundity symbols in ancient China," BMFEA, No. 2.

C34 "Notes on the history of Chinese popular literature" in *T'oung Pao*, Vol. XXVIII, 1931, p. 346–54.

Deals with Fēng Mēng-lung (1574/5–1645/6), the *Chin Ku Ch'i Kuan*, Ling Mēng-ch'u and Chin Shēng-t'an.

C35 "An eleventh century correspondence" in *Etudes d'Orientalisme publiées par le Musée Guimet à la mémoire de Raymonde Linossier*, 2 Vols., Paris, 1932, Vol. II, p. 531–62.

Partial translation of the *Higashiyama Orai* (c. 1100) and its supplement. As A.W. says in his introduction, the work is a collection of letters and replies between a priest and his flock dealing mostly with Buddhist ritual, doctrine and iconography. Some other, more general, matters are discussed, such as medicine and other, non-Buddhist, cults.

For the importance of this text in matters of iconography, see A20, p. xix.

C36 "References to Alchemy in Buddhist scriptures" in *Bulletin of the School of Oriental Studies*, Vol. VI, Pt. IV, 1932, p. 1102–3.

"A supplement to my 'Notes on Chinese alchemy.' " (*q.v.*, C31).

C37 "Did Buddha die of eating pork? with a note on Buddha's image" in *Mélanges Chinois et Bouddhiques*, Vol. I, Bruxelles, July 1932, p. 343–54.

Discusses the word *sūkaramaddava* and the change in the view about meat-eating which appears to have taken place about the third century. A.W. calls attention to the fact that a definite embargo on the representation of Buddha is referred to in the Chinese *Tripitaka*.

C38 "New light on Buddhism in medieval India" in *Mélanges Chinois et Bouddhiques*, Vol. I, Bruxelles, July 1932, p. 355–76.

Translation of a document, on a stupa at the Juniper Rock Temple in Korea (printed in the *Taishō Tripitaka*, Vol. LI, p. 982), by Li Se, c. 1377, in memory of the Indian priest Dhyānabhadra, which shows that Buddhism survived in India Propter at the beginning of the fourteenth century to a greater extent than previously supposed. The question is raised whether many aspects of Zen, previously regarded as originating in China, did not have their beginnings in India.

C39 "The Book of Changes" in *Bulletin of the Museum of Far Eastern Antiquities*, Stockholm, No. 5, 1933, p. 121–42.

A.W. theorises that the *Book of Changes* is an amalgam of two quite separate works: an omen, or "peasant interpretation" text, and a divination text of later date and more sophisticated nature.

C40 "Kono Tabi: a little known Japanese religion" in *Bulletin of the School of Oriental Studies*, Vol. VII, Pt. I, 1933, p. 105–9.

Re-printed in **A40**.

C41 "Note on the word *chiao* [徼]" in *Bulletin of the School of Oriental Studies*, Vol. VII, Pt. III, 1934, p. 717–18.

C42 with C. H. Armbruster, "The verb 'to say' as an auxiliary in Africa and China" in *Bulletin of the School of Oriental Studies*, Vol. VII, Pt. III, 1934, p. 573–76.

C43 "The Eclipse poem and its group" in *T'ien Hsia Monthly*, Oct. 1936, p. 245–48.

Discusses the dating of certain political laments in the *Book of Songs* to 735 B.C. instead of 776 B.C. A.W. omitted these poems from his translation of *The Book of Songs*, (**A25**, *q.v.*).

C44 "Waiting for the new" in *The New Statesman*, July 10, 1937, p. 71.

Article on the hold which ski-ing has on its devotees.

C44a "Mystics and Scholars" in *The Aryan Path*, Sept. 1937, p. 399–400.

Points out the value of scholarship to the mystic.

C45 "Chuang Tzu and Hui Tzu: intuition versus intellect" in E. R. Hughes, *China body and soul*, London, 1938, p. 157–66.

Re-printed in *Three Ways* . . . (**A27**), p. 17–24.

C46 "The Lucky stone and the Lung stone" in *Bulletin of the School of Oriental Studies*, Vol. IX, Pt. 3, 1938, p. 729–32.

Deals with two passages from the *Chou Li* and the possibility of there having been a megalithic culture in China.

C47 "Our debt to China" in *The Asiatic Review*, July 1940, p. 554–57.

Mainly concerns Hsü Chi-mo (d. 1931), who interpreted many of the good things about England to the Chinese during the inter-war years.

C47a "Animals in Chinese Art" in *The Listener*, June 10, 1943, p. 698.

Some comments upon a London exhibition and its catalogue.

C47b "Roger Fry" in *The Listener*, Aug. 15, 1940, p. 243.

Contains some remarks on Virginia Woolf's *Roger Fry*, London, 1940.

C48 "The Japanese spirit" in *The New Statesman*, Oct. 16, 1943, p. 247.

Speaks of the change in meaning, throughout Japanese history, of the expression *Yamato-damashii*, 'Japanese spirit.'

C49 "Sir William Jones as sinologue" in *Bulletin of the School of Oriental Studies*, Vol. XI, Pt. 4, 1946, p. 842.

Sir William (1746–1794) concerned himself chiefly with Indian studies.

C50 "The Chinese Cinderella Story" in *Folk-Lore*, Vol. LVIII, Mar. 1947, p. 226–38.

A.W. puts on record, together with some comments, the earliest datable version of the Cinderella story, from Tuan Ch'êng-shih's *Yu Yang Tsa Tsu*, c. A.D. 850–860. An Appendix of three other foreign stories recorded by Tuan—"A Korean story," "Turkic story" and "The King of Persia's daughter" (for this latter, *v.* A34)—is included. The whole article was re-printed in **A40**.

C51 "More than a revival" in *The New Statesman*, Mar. 8, 1947, p. 152.

Notice of the ballet *Boutique Fantasque*, performed at Covent Garden.

C52 "China's greatest writer: Arthur Waley on Han Yü" in *The Listener*, May 22, 1947, p. 799–800.

Transcription of a broadcast talk on China's greatest prose writer. Re-printed in **A40**.

C52a "Social Organisation in Ancient China" in *The Modern Quarterly*, N.S. Vol. 2, No. 3, Summer 1947, p. 208–14.

"The following notes are based on information collected while preparing a biography of the Chinese poet Po Chü-i . . ."

C53 "The early years of Po Chü-i" in *The Cornhill Magazine*, No. 973, Winter 1947–48, p. 57–71.

The first chapter of A.W.'s biography of the poet (**A31**, *q.v.*).

C54 "A Note on Edith Sitwell's poetry" in A *Celebration for Edith Sitwell* . . . edited by José Garcia Villa, (*Direction Seven*), Norfolk, Conn., 1948, p. 83–89.

". . . I have chosen in this note chiefly to discuss her technique and material, fully aware that in doing so I am merely skirting the periphery of her art." (p. 84)

A.W. finds a certain poverty in Edith Sitwell's re-creation of myth in poems which were recently published when he wrote his note.

C55 "Note on Iron and the Plough in early China" in *Bulletin of the School of Oriental Studies*, Vol. XII, Pts. 3 and 4, 1948, p. 803–4.

A.W. gives his reasons for questioning the currently accepted dates of two landmarks in cultural history.

C56 "Confucianism and the virtues of Moderation" in *The Listener*, Feb. 26, 1948, p. 349–50.

No. 2 in a series of broadcast talks on world religions.

C56a "Music and Dancing in the works of Po Chü-i" in *Ballet*, Vol. 5, No. 3, March 1948, p. 33–39.

Subsequently appeared in *The Life and Times* . . . (A31), p. 150–56.

C56b "Gedichte als Prüfstein: Aufnahmenprüfungen für den Staatsdienst zur Zeit der T'ang-dynastie" in *Neue Auslese*, Heft 7, July 1948, p. 28–31.

Appears at greater length in A31, p. 16–24.

C57 "Notes on Mencius" in *Asia Major*, N.S. Vol. I, 1949, p. 99–108.

"The following notes, then, deal with the principal passages where Legge [in his translation of Mencius, 1861] is certainly wrong, and with a few other points of script or grammar." (p. 99) Re-printed, with an extra comment, as part of the material added to the 1960 edition of *The Chinese Classics*, Vol. II.

C58 "The fall of Lo-yang" in *History Today*, April 1951, p. 7–10.

A general account of the city and of the people who lived in it at the time of the sack of A.D. 311. Re-printed in **A40**.

C59 "A Chinese poet in Central Asia" in *History Today*, Nov. 1951, p. 7–15.

Biography of Ts'ên Shên, A.D. 715–770, with translations of eleven of his poems. Re-printed in **A40**.

C60 "Anquetil-Duperron and Sir William Jones" in *History Today*, Jan. 1952, p. 23–33.

Biography of the translator of the *Zend Avesta*, whom Jones accused of fraud. A.-D. later translated 51 Upanishads which had some influence on Schopenhauer. Re-printed in **A40**.

C61 "Life under the Han dynasty: Notes on Chinese civilization in the First and Second Centuries A.D." in *History Today*, Feb. 1953, p. 89–98.

Seven illustrations from *Han tomb art of Western China*, by R. C. Rudolph and Wen Yu, 1951.

C62 "Texts from China and Japan," Fourth part of *Buddhist texts through the ages*, E. Conze ed., Oxford, 1954, p. 271–306.

Introduction [A.W.'s criteria for his selection].
Texts originating in India.
The Parable of Me and Mine, *Takakusu Tripitaka*, Vol. XV, p. 211.
On the curing of illness contracted during Dhyāna practice, TT, Vol. XV, p. 333.
Meditation upon the Element Water, TT, Vol. XV, p. 328.

Judging the Character of a Dhyāna Pupil, *TT*, Vol. XV, p. 270c.

The Bracelets, *TT*, Vol. XV, p. 281.

All Words are true, *TT*, Vol. XV, p. 50 and 82.

Buddha's Doctrine, *TT*, Vol. XV, p. 39 and 70.

The Negation of Dhyāna, *TT*, Vol. IX, p. 368.

On reading the Dhyāna Sutra, Poem by Po Chü-i.

Nationality, *TT*, Vol. XV, p. 274.

The Intermediate State, *TT*, Vol. XVII, p. 200c.

Devas re-people the Earth, *TT*, Vol. II, p. 737 and Vol. I, p. 362.

Buddha's Pity, *TT*, Vol. XXIV, p. 1036.

Texts originating in China and Japan.

A Hinayana sect in Early China.

The Truly So, *TT*, Vol. XXXII, p. 576.

From the Lives of the Nuns [Ching-chien, Seng-kuo, Feng], *TT*, Vol. L, p. 934, 939, 946.

On Trust in the Heart, *TT*, Vol. XLVIII, p. 376.

From the Conversations of Shen-hui, J. Gernet, *Entretiens du Maître de Dhyāna Chen-houei*, Hanoi, 1949.

A Nice Mountain, *TT*, Vol. LI, p. 255.

Rain-making, *San Tendai Godaisan Ki.*

In addition A.W. translated Hsüan-tsang's version of the *Mahāprajñāpāramitā* for the second part of the book (p. 154–58).

C62a "The Art of Utamaro: Arthur Waley on the exhibition at the British Museum" in *The Listener*, Jan. 7, 1954, p. 61.

C63 "The poetry of Chinese mirrors" in *The Listener*, Oct. 7, 1954, p. 565–66.

A.W. gives some examples of poems, stories and inscriptions dealing with the part that metal mirrors played in Chinese literature and popular belief. Transcription of a broadcast. Re-printed in **A40**.

C64 "The heavenly Horses of Ferghana: a new view" in *History Today*, Feb. 1955, p. 95–103.

The religious importance of the horses brought back from Ta Yüan after the expedition of 102 B.C. emphasised by A.W. in contrast with the traditional view of their military importance. See **B7** for Tu Fu's use of the *Song of the heavenly horse*.

C65 "History and Religion" in *Philosophy East and West*, April 1955, p. 75–78.

A note on the exchange of views between D. T. Suzuki and Hu Shih published in the April 1953 number of *Philosophy East and West*. Re-printed in A40.

C66 "Dreams and their interpretation: Arthur Waley on some oriental theories" in *The Listener*, May 26, 1955, p. 931–32.

A broadcast talk. Re-printed in J. Morris, *From the Third Programme*, London, 1956, p. 222–31 and in A40.

C67 "A lost ballad by Po Chü-i" in *Sino-Japonica, Festschrift André Wedemeyer*, Leipzig, 1956, p. 213–14.

A.W. quotes two couplets of "The sorrows of Miss Jên" from Ōye Koretoki's *Senzai Kaku* c. 950, and gives a short commentary.

C68 "Some references to Iranian temples in the Tun-huang region" in *Bulletin of the Institute of History and Philology, Academia Sinica*, Vol. XXVIII, Studies presented to Hu Shih on his sixty-fifth birthday, Part 1, Taipei, 1956, p. 123–28.

A commentary on five texts relating to Iranian cults which A.W. collected from the Tun-huang MSS. He suggests that Sung references to Iranians at K'ai-fêng and Lo-yang (as mentioned in Tung Yu's *Kuang-chüan Hua Po*) might be usefully investigated.

C69 "Stories of Chinese ghosts" in *The Listener*, Mar. 22, 1956, p. 286–88.

A broadcast talk. Re-printed in **A40**.

C70 "Commodore Anson at Canton: a Chinese account" in *History Today*, April 1956, p. 274–77.

This article, in almost identical form, also appeared as Appendix I in *Yuan Mei* (**A37**, *q.v.*). A.W. translates Yuan Mei's account of Anson's visit in 1743.

C71 "Chinese-Mongol hybrid songs" in *Bulletin of the School of Oriental Studies*, Vol. XX, 1957, p. 581–84.

Discussion of the anonymous (fourteenth century?) song-sequence called "The Hunt" (*Tz'ŭ-lin Chai-yen*).

C72 "The Green Bower Collection" in *Oriental Art*, Vol. III, 1957, p. 50–54 and 107–9.

Introduction to, and translation of parts of, Hsia Po-ho's *Ch'ing Lou Chi* (c. 1364), a series of notes upon the careers of about a hundred singing girls, of whom approximately half performed in regular drama. Re-printed in **A40**.

C73 "Chinese stories about actors" in *The Listener*, Feb. 7, 1957, p. 223–24.

A broadcast talk, re-printed in **A40**.

C74 "A legend about the Caves of the myriad Buddhas" in *Sino-Indian Studies*, Vol. V, Pts. 3 and 4, May 1957, p. 241–42.

A tale from the collection, made by Yuan Mei, called *Tzu pu yü*. The story appears in A.W.'s *Yuan Mei* (A37), p. 135–36, where eleven others from the collection and its supplement are translated.

C75 "Notes on translation" in *The Atlantic Monthly*, Nov. 1958, p. 107–12.

"These scattered notes on translation deal principally with the Far East, because that is where my own experience lies" (p. 112). In addition to being illuminating on A.W.'s methods and opinions, the article contains a discussion of the work of the Chinese translator Lin Shu (1852–1924). Re-printed in A40.

C76 "Notes on the *Tun-huang Pien-wên Chi*" in *Studia Serica Bernhard Karlgren dedicata*, Copenhagen, 1959, p. 172–77.

Comments on some 42 textual problems in the edition which A.W. used for his *Ballads and Stories . . .* (A39).

C77 "Notes on the *Yüan-ch'ao pi-shih*" in *Bulletin of the School of Oriental Studies*, Vol. XXIII, 1960, p. 523–29.

Comments on a dozen points in the text of the Chinese version of *The Secret History of the Mongols*. In its present form it must be dated later than 1258.

C78 "A Memory of Yoshio Makino" in *Orient/West*, July 1961, p. 15–16.

A brief note on Makino (d. 1956) as A.W. knew him between 1919 and 1923.

C79 "Chinese" in *Eos: An Enquiry into the theme of Lovers' Meetings and Partings at Dawn in Poetry*, A. T. Hatto ed., The Hague, 1965, p. 107–113.

"Japanese" in *Eos* . . . p. 114–25.

A.W. wrote two sections of this comparative study of the *alba*, using a few examples drawn from his own works, though the majority of the poems he had not previously translated.

C80 "Colloquial in the Yu-hsien k'u" in *Bulletin of the School of Oriental Studies*, Vol. XXIX, 1966, p. 559–65.

A review article of H. S. Levy's translation (*The Dwelling of playful goddesses*, Tokyo, 1965), of the T'ang story gives A.W. the opportunity to make suggestions on the rendering of some of the colloquial expressions.

D: ORIGINAL POETRY AND PROSE

D1 "Carbonari Ball" [*Poem*] in *Basileon* △, June 1909, p. 20.

Unsigned. The Carbonari was the name of a society founded by Hugh Dalton and Rupert Brooke at King's College, Cambridge, in 1906. Christopher Hassall's *Rupert Brooke*, 1964, gives some information concerning the group, of which A.W. became a member when he went to King's from Rugby.

D2 "Change" [*Poem*] in *Basileon* △, June 1909, p. 20.

Unsigned.

D3 "German Outskirts" [*Poem*] in *The Cambridge Review*, Vol. 34, Feb. 27, 1913, p. 319.

Signed A. D. Schloss.

D4 "The Presentation" in *The Nation*, May 24, 1924, p. 244.

Short story. Re-printed in A40.

D5 "Et pourtant c'est triste quand meurent les empires" [*Poem*] in *The New Statesman*, Nov. 23, 1940, p. 513.

D6 "Censorship: a poem in the Chinese style" in *Horizon*, Vol. II, Dec. 1940, p. 287.

Dedicated to Hsiao Ch'ien. Unsigned. Re-printed under A.W.'s name in *The Golden Horizon*, edited by Cyril Connolly, London, 1953, p. 19–20, and in A40. Hsiao dedicated his *The Dragon*

Beards versus the Blueprints, 1944, jointly to E. M. Forster and A.W. See also **G10**.

D6a "Books in Bloomsbury" [*Poem*] in *The Listener*, Feb. 20, 1941, p. 264.

D7 "No discharge" [*Poem*] in *The New Statesman*, July 12, 1941, p. 34.

A slightly differing version was printed in *The New Republic*, Dec. 1, 1941, p. 731. Re-printed in **A40**.

D7a "Swan" in *The Listener*, July 24, 1941, p. 123.

The poem was re-printed, in slightly differing form, in **A40**.

D8 "Intellectual conversation" in *The Abinger Chronicle*, Vol. 4, No. 4, Aug.–Sept. 1943, p. 34–37.

Reminiscences, written for Beryl de Zoete, of A.W.'s Cambridge friends, dated Autumn 1940.

D9 "Monkey. *A new chapter by Arthur Waley, dedicated to Violet Gordon Woodhouse, in gratitude for fairy music*" in *The Cornhill Magazine*, Vol. 161, Dec. 1945, p. 434–45.

An original addition to *Monkey* (*v.* **A29**), re-printed in, *The Real Tripitaka* (**A34**).

D10 "The Dragon Cup" in *The Cornhill Magazine*, Vol. 162, Autumn 1946, p. 121–27.

Short story, re-printed in *The Real Tripitaka* (**A34**).

D11 "In the Gallery" in *The Cornhill Magazine*, Vol. 163, Winter 1948–49, p. 367–73.

Short story. First appeared in a privately printed edition, **A30a**; re-printed in **A40**.

D12 "The King of Death" in *Rider's Review*, Vol. 76, 1949–50, p. 25–28.

A fable, re-printed as "The King of the Dead" in *The Real Tripitaka* (**A34**).

E: BOOK REVIEWS

This listing of A.W.'s reviews would have been considerably augmented by putting on record his numerous contributions to the *Times Literary Supplement* between 1920 and 1958, had access to the files been granted. In order to show Dr. Waley's connexion with the *Literary Supplement,* one important article has been selected.

The place of publication of a book reviewed is London unless otherwise stated. The titles of well-known periodicals have been abbreviated after the first citation.

E1 Couling, S. *The Encyclopaedia Sinica,* 1917, in *Bulletin of the School of Oriental Studies,* 1918, p. 144–45.

A.W. contributed notes on painting and poetry.

E2 Koop, A. J., and Inada, H. *Japanese names: a manual for students and art collectors,* Part I, 1920, in *BSOS,* Pt. IV, 1920, p. 180–81.

E3 Rosthorn, A. *Die Anfänge der Chinesischen Geschichtschreibung,* Wien, 1920, in *Journal of the Royal Asiatic Society,* Oct. 1921, p. 662.

E4 *Chinesische Schattenspiele,* Hrsg. von Wilhelm Grube u. Emil Krebs, Leipzig, 1915, in *JRAS,* Oct. 1921, p. 662–63.

E5 "Chinese Historians" in *Times Literary Supplement,* Mar. 9, 1922, p. 145–46.

Discursive review of Henri Cordier's *Histoire Générale de la Chine*, 1920–21, allows A.W. to point out the errors into which most Western historians of China have fallen in their use of sources, and to suggest the remedy—increased use of the *Chēng shih* rather than the *Pien nien*.

E6 Anesaki, M. *Quelques pages de l'histoire religieuse du Japon* . . . , Paris, 1921, in *JRAS*, Jan. 1923, p. 124.

E7 Ardenne de Tizac, J. H. d'. *Animals in Chinese Art*, 1923, in *Burlington Magazine*, May 1923, p. 215–16.

E8 Reichwein, A. *China und Europa im 18 Jahrhundert*, Berlin, 1923, in *New Statesman*, July 7, 1923, p. 396–97.

E9 *Ergebnisse der Königlichen Preussischen Turfan-Expeditionen* . . . , von A. von Le Coq, Berlin, 1923, in *BSOS*, 1924, p. 342–45.

E10 Karlgren, B. *Analytic dictionary of Chinese and Sino-Japanese*, Paris, 1923, in *BSOS*, 1924, p. 362–65.

E11 Obata, S. *The Works of Li Po*, 1923, in *New Republic*, Jan. 16, 1924.

E12 Ohasama, S. *Zen: Der lebendige Buddhismus in Japan*, Berlin, 1925, in *Artibus Asiae*, 1925, p. 237–39.

E13 "A Note on two new studies of Chinese Mythology" in *Man*, Sept. 1925, p. 133–34.

Remarks on O. Manchen-Helfen, "The later books of the Shen-hai-king" in *Asia Major*, 1924, p. 550–86, and A. Forke, *The world conception of the Chinese*, 1925.

E14 *Chin ku ch'i kuan: the inconstancy of Madam Chuang and other stories from the Chinese*, translated by E. B. Howell, 1924, in *NS*, April 11, 1925.

E15 "Allusion as an element in Poetry" in *NS*, Aug. 22, 1925.

Reviews of R. Kōda, *Leaving the Hermitage*, 1925, and A. S. Lee, tr., *Flower Shadows*, 1925.

E16 Keiki, Y. *Sankai Kyō no Kenkyū: an investigation concerning the Three Degrees sect*, Tokyo, 1927, in *BSOS*, 1928, p. 162–69.

"The most important work on the Tun-huang manuscripts since *Un Traité Manichéen retrouvé en Chine*, by Pelliot and Chavannes."

E17 Chanoch, A. *Die Altjapanische Jahreszeiten Poesie aus dem Kokinshū*, Leipzig, 1928, in *BSOS*, 1929, p. 655.

E18 Godard, A., *et al. Les Antiquités Bouddhiques de Bāmiyān*, T. II, Paris, 1928, in *Antiquity*, June 1930, p. 257–58.

E19 Hamada, K. *Pi-tzu-wo: Prehistoric sites by the river Pu-liu-ho, South Manchuria*, Tokyo, 1929, in *Antiquity*, June 1930, p. 262.

E20 Le Coq, A. von., *Buried Treasures of Chinese Turkestan*, 1929, in *Antiquity*, June 1930, p. 261.

E21 Marchal, H. *Guide archéologique aux temples d'Angkor*, Paris, 1928, in *Antiquity*, June 1930, p. 259.

E22 Stein, Sir A. *On Alexander's track to the Indus*, 1929, in *Antiquity*, June 1930, p. 269.

E23 Barthoux, J. J. *Les fouilles de Haḍḍa*, T. III, Paris, 1930, in *Antiquity*, Mar. 1931, p. 134–35.

Haḍḍa the Hsi-lo (Hela) of the Chinese Buddhist pilgrims.

E24 Ghosh, M. *Rock-paintings and other antiquities of prehistoric and later times*, Calcutta, 1932, in *Antiquity*, March 1933, p. 128.

E25 Museum of Far Eastern Antiquities, Stockholm, *Bulletin*, No. 3, 1931, in *Antiquity*, March 1933, p. 128.

E26 Glathe, A. *Die Chinesischen Zahlen*, Leipzig, 1932, in *JRAS*, April 1933, p. 439.

E27 Katō, G. *Le Shinto* . . . , Paris, 1931, in *JRAS*, April 1933, p. 438.

E28 Yetts, W. P. *The George Eumofopoulos collection* . . . *Vol III, Buddhist Sculpture*, 1932, in *JRAS*, April 1933, p. 440–42.

"It is indeed the best general account of the beginnings of Buddhism and Buddhist culture that has yet appeared."

E29 Shah, C. J. *Jainism in Northern India . . .* , 1932, in *Antiquity*, June 1933, p. 256.

E30 Buck, P. *All Men are Brothers*, 1933, in *New Republic*, Nov. 22, 1933, p. 51.

E31 Barthoux, J. J. *Les fouilles de Haḍḍa*, T. IV, Paris, 1933, and
Hackin, J. *L'œuvre de la délégation archéologique française en Afghanistan* (1922–32), Vol. I, Tokyo, 1933, in *Antiquity*, Sept. 1934, p. 359.

E32 Eliot, Sir C. *Japanese Buddhism*, 1935, in *NS*, April 6, 1935, p. 496.

E33 Evans-Wentz, W. Y. *Tibetan Yoga and secret doctrines*, 1935, in *NS*, Sept. 14, 1935, p. 348.

E34 Yoshitake, S. *The Phonetic system of ancient Japanese*, 1934, in *JRAS*, Oct. 1935, p. 771–72.

E35 Tun Li-ch'en. *Annual Customs and festivals in Peking . . .* , translated and annotated by Derk Bodde, Peiping, 1936, in *Folk-Lore*, Dec. 1936, p. 402–3.

E36 Chikashige, M. *Alchemy and other chemical achievements of the ancient Orient*, Tokyo, 1936, in *Folk-Lore*, Mar. 1938, p. 100.

E37 Chinese Folk-Lore Society. *Journal of Chinese Folk-Lore*, Vol. I, No. 2, Jan. 1937, in *Man*, April 1938, p. 62–63.

E38 Sirén, O. A *History of later Chinese Painting*, 1938, in *NS*, July 23, 1938, p. 164.

E39 Irving, R. L. G. *The Alps*, 1939, and
Smythe, F. S. A *Camera in the hills*, 1939, in *NS*, Dec. 23, 1939, p. 934.

E40 Gardner, C. S. *Chinese traditional historiography*, Cambridge (Mass.), 1938, in *JRAS*, Jan. 1940, p. 81–82.

Points out a few inaccuracies and the omission of the inscriptions on early bronzes.

E41 Unwin, J. D. *Hopousia, or the sexual and economic foundations of a new society*, 1940, in *NS*, May 4, 1940, p. 598.

E42 Yetts, W. P. *The Cull Chinese bronzes*, 1939, in *JRAS*, June 1940, p. 227–31.

Discusses some inscriptional characters on the interpretation of which A.W. differed from Yetts.

E43 Hardy, G. H. A *Mathematician's apology*, 1940, in *NS*, Feb. 15, 1941.

E44 Peck, G. *Through China's wall*, 1941, and
Crow, C. *Foreign Devils in the Flowery Kingdom*, 1941, in *NS*, Mar. 29, 1941, p. 334 and 336.

E45 Chiang Yee. *The silent traveller in the Yorkshire Dales*, 1941, and
Fitzgerald, C. P. *The Tower of five glories*, 1941, in *NS*, May 17, 1941, p. 514.

E46 Lin Yutang. *With love and irony,* 1941, in NS, June 28, 1941, p. 656.

E47 Lattimore, O. *Mongol Journeys,* 1941, in NS, Aug. 9, 1941, p. 142.

E48 Collis, M. *The great within,* 1941, in NS, Dec. 6, 1941, p. 477–78.

E49 Chadwick, N. K. *Poetry and Prophecy,* 1942, in NS, Mar. 14, 1942, p. 180.

E50 Lunn, A. *Mountain Jubilee,* 1943, in NS, Oct. 23, 1943, p. 274.

E51 Sitwell, O. *Sing high! Sing low!,* 1944, in NS, Aug. 12, 1944, p. 109.

E52 Wang, C. C., *ed. Readings in traditional Chinese,* New York, 1944,
Daniels, O. *Dictionary of Japanese Sōsho writing forms,* 1944,
Daniels, F. J., *ed. Japanese prose: texts and translations,* 1944,
Henderson, H. *Handbook of Japanese grammar,* 1945, in BSOS, 1947, p. 261–62.

E53 Cohn, W. *Chinese Painting,* 1948, in *The Listener,* July 29, 1948, p. 172.

E54   Collis, M. *The First holy one*, 1948, in *NS*, Aug. 14, 1948, p. 140.

E55   Liebenthal, W. *The book of Chao*, Peking, 1948, in *JRAS*, 1950, p. 80.

E56   Lin Li-kouang. *L'aide-mémoire de la vraie loi*, Paris, 1949, in *JRAS*, 1950, p. 87.

E57   *Po Hu T'ung* (*The comprehensive discussions in the White Tiger Hall*), Vol. I, Leiden, 1949, and *K'ung Tzŭ Chia Yü* (*The School sayings of Confucius*), Leiden, 1950, in *JRAS*, 1950, p. 194–95.

E58   Gernet, J. *Entretiens du Maître de Dhyāna Chen-Houei du Ho-Tsö*, Hanoi, 1949, in *JRAS*, 1951, p. 208.

E59   Hightower, J. *Topics in Chinese literature*, Cambridge (Mass.), 1950, in *JRAS*, 1951, p. 114.

E60   Hoffmann, A. *Die Lieder des Li Yü*, Cologne, 1950, in *JRAS*, 1951, p. 110 .

E61   Petech, L. *Northern India according to the Shui-ching-chu*, Rome, 1950, in *JRAS*, 1951, p. 113.

E62   Swann, N. L. *Food and money in Ancient China*, Princeton, 1950, in *JRAS*, 1951, p. 114.

E63   Keene, D. *The Battles of Coxinga: Chikamatsu's puppet play* . . . 1951, in *JRAS*, 1952, p. 92. (with C. R. Boxer)

E64 Boxer, C. R. *The Christian century in Japan*, Berkeley, 1951, in *JRAS*, 1952, p. 159–60.

E65 Pelliot, P. *Notes sur l'histoire de la Horde d'Or*, Paris, 1949, in *JRAS*, 1952, p. 172–73.

E66 Dumoulin, H. *The development of Chinese Zen after the Sixth Patriarch . . .* New York, 1953, in *Artibus Asiae*, 1954, p. 75–76.

E67 Hamilton, R. H., ed. *Buddhism . . . selections from Buddhist literature*, New York, 1952, in *Artibus Asiae*, 1954, p. 76–77.

E68 T'ao Ch'ien. *The Poems*, translated by Lily Pao-hu Chang and Marjorie Sinclair, Honolulu, 1953, in *Artibus Asiae*, 1954, p. 178–80.

E69 Wright, A. F. *Studies in Chinese thought*, New York, 1953, in *Artibus Asiae*, 1954, p. 71.

E69a *Ethnographische Beiträge aus der Ch'inghai Provinz, China*, Peking, 1952, in *Folk-Lore*, Sept. 1954, p. 115–16.

E70 Oka, K. *Genji Monogatari no Kisoteki Kenkyū*, Tokyo, 1954, in *BSOS*, 1955, p. 387.

E71 Pulleyblank, E. J. *The background of the rebellion of An Lu-shan*, 1955, in *JRAS*, 1955, p. 174–76.

E72   Chang Chung-li. *The Chinese gentry*, Seattle, 1955, in *JRAS*, 1956, p. 94–95.

E73   Nagao, G. M. *A study of Tibetan Buddhism*, Tokyo, 1954, in *JRAS*, 1956, p. 93–94.

E74   Tsukamoto, Z., ed. *Chōron-kenkyu* [*Studies in the Chao-lun*], Kyoto, 1955, in *BSOS*, 1957, p. 195–96.

E75   Gripekoven, J. *Confucius et son temps*, Brussels, 1955, and
     Liu Wu-chi *Confucius: his life and time*, 1956, in *Journal of Asian Studies*, Feb. 1957, p. 298–300.

E76   Kaizuka, S. *Confucius*, 1956, in *JAS*, Nov. 1957, p. 140.

E77   Mishima, Y. *Five modern Nō plays*, New York, 1957, in *JAS*, May 1958, p. 487.

E78   Zach, E. v. *Die Chinesische Anthologie*, Cambridge (Mass.), Rpt. 1958, in *BSOS*, 1959, p. 383–84.

E79   Grousset, R. *Chinese art and culture*, 1959, in *The Listener*, Feb. 18, 1960, p. 313–14.

E80   Wright, A. F. *Buddhism in Chinese history*, Stanford, 1959, in *BSOS*, 1960, p. 428.

E81 *The Book of Lieh-tzu,* translated by A. C. Graham, 1961, in *The Sunday Times* (London), Jan. 22, 1961, p. 26.

E82 Wilhelm, H. *Change: Eight lectures on the I Ching,* 1961, in *The Listener,* Mar. 30, 1961, p. 579–80.

E83 Watson, W. *China before the Han dynasty,* 1961, in *The Sunday Times* (London), Oct. 22, 1961, p. 31.

F: MISCELLANEOUS

Fa1 "Preface to the Epidendrum-Pagoda collection," MS.   2½ p.

A.W.'s translation of Wang Hsi-chih's *Preface* accompanied a letter to Sir Sydney Cockerell dated Mar. 16, 1916. Both are now in the possession of Mr. A. R. A. Hobson. Versions can be found in: Zottoli, A. *Cursus litterae sinicae*, 1879–1909, Vol. IV, p. 295–97, Grube, W. *Geschichte der chinesischen literatur*, 1902, p. 253–54, and Margouliès, G. *Le Kou-wen*, 1926, p. 126–28. See also A.W.'s *An Introduction* . . . (A9), p. 70.

F1 "Mr. Waley on the T'ao Ch'ien poem" in *Poetry*, Vol. XIV, No. I, April 1919, p. 55–56.

Letter from A.W. dated Feb. 20, 1919, suggesting two emendations in Florence Ayscough's translation of T'ao Ch'ien's "On the Classic of the hills and sea," published in *Poetry*, Vol. XIII, No. V, Feb. 1919, p. 239.

F2 "A word from Mr. Waley" in *Poetry*, Vol. XVI, No. II, Nov. 1920, p. 103–4.

A reply to Jun Fujita's review of A.W.'s *Japanese Poetry* in *Poetry*, Vol. XVI, No. V, Aug. 1920, p. 283–87.

F2a *Callimachus*, a play translated from Hroswitha's (10th cent.) Latin text by A.W., was performed at the Haymarket Theatre on Dec. 7, 1920, by the Art Theatre.

Unpublished.

F2a1 Luce, G. H. *Journal of the Burma Research Society*, Vol. 14, 1924, p. 87–205 and Vol. 15, p. 115–28. A collection, in two untitled articles, of passages in the

Chinese histories dealing with the early history of Burma. Luce acknowledges A.W.'s contribution of some newly translated material.

F2b Yashiro, Yukio. *Sandro Botticelli* . . . London, 1925.

A.W.'s assistance acknowledged in the Preface.

F3 "The Imperial Secretary on the occasion of a Burmese pwe at the Chinese court, A.D. 802."

Translation of a poem by Po Chü-i, contributed to: Harvey, G. E., *History of Burma*, London, 1925, p. 14–15. For Po's attitude to music, see *The Life and Times* . . . (A31), p. 150.

F4 *The Year Book of Oriental Art and Culture, 1924–1925, Edited by Arthur Waley*, London, 1925 [*No more published*], contains, by A.W.:

"Yün Shou-p'ing, called 'Nan-t'ien,' 1633–1690," p. 1–3. Illustrates one of the flower-painter's works, a nine-fold screen painted on silk.

"The Tsun Shēng Pa Chien, A.D. 1591," translated by A.W. with an introduction and notes by R. L. Hobson, p. 80–87. Kao Lien's remarks about the classic wares of the Sung dynasty were included in the K'ang Hsi encyclopaedia. The article is followed by an Appendix, a translation of Su Tung-p'o's "Making Tea in the Examination Hall."

F5 *Kai Khosru Monographs on Eastern Art*, General Editor, Arthur Waley. Published in this series were:

Pierce, H., and Tyler, R. *Byzantine Art*, London, 1926.
Borovka, G. *Scythian Art*, London, 1928.
Harcourt-Smith, S. *Babylonian Art*, London, 1928.

F6 Wilhelm, R. *The Soul of China*, London, 1928.

A.W. translated the poems in the book.

F6a Woolf, V. *Orlando*, London, 1928.

Acknowledges A.W.'s help.

F7 Firbank, R. *The Works of Ronald Firbank*, 5 vols., London, 1929.

Introduction by A.W., Vol. I, p. 1–11. "Firbank, then, is important because he is the first and almost the only Impressionist in English fiction, the earliest writer . . . to do in writing what Cezanne, Matisse, Renoir did in painting." (p. 3)
"This essay is frankly a eulogy. It has been my business to point out the merits of Firbank's work. To its defects—above all to its frequent incoherence and lack of construction—I am not blind." (p. 11)

F8 Ts'ao Hsüeh-ch'in and Kao Ngoh. *The Dream of the Red Chamber*, New York, 1929.

A.W.'s preface to Professor Wang's translation and adaptation appears on p. vii–xiii. He discusses the position of fiction in Chinese literature and the reasons for the failure to develop a technique of novel writing comparable to that of the West. He points out that the method of the "open air proletarian story-teller" has affected the *Hung Lou Mêng*. See also **F20**.

F9 Seligman, C. G. "Chinese socketed celts" in *Antiquity*, Vol. XII, 1938, p. 86–87.

Acknowledges A.W.'s help in establishing the existence of the socketed celt in China in Shang-Yin times.

F10 de Zoete, B. *Dance and Drama in Bali*, London, 1938.

A.W., in his preface (p. xvii–xx), commends this special study of an individual dance-area as being an essential pre-requisite to a synthesis on the evolution of the drama.

F11   *Chin P'ing Mei,* London, 1939.

A.W. contributed an introduction (p. ix–xxii) in which he deals with: The legend of the *Chin P'ing Mei,* the facts about the *Chin P'ing Mei,* the *Chin P'ing Mei* and the censorship, and the milieu which produced the *Chin P'ing Mei.* He regards Hsü Wei as the strongest of the possible candidates for the authorship of the book.

F12   Archer, W. G. *The Blue grove: the poetry of the Uraons,* London, 1940.

After mentioning the importance as literature of Archer's translations of the traditional songs, A.W. calls attention to the small amount of work done by ethnologists on unwritten poetry and commends the author for showing how song is bound up with other activities (Foreword, p. 7–10).

F13   Acton, H., and Lee Yi-hsieh. *Glue and Lacquer: four cautionary tales,* London, 1941.

In his preface (p. vii–xi) to the tales, taken from a collection called *Hsing Shih Hêng Yen,* published in 1627 by Fêng Mênglung (see also **C34**), A.W. gives a brief biography of Fêng, discusses Chinese colloquial literature and compares it with Western fiction. The original sub-title of the book was used as the title of the second edition when John Lehmann published it in 1947.

F14   Koo, T. Z. *Folk songs from China . . . English text by Irene Gass and Arthur Waley . . .* London, 1943.

A.W. translated two of the songs for this collection, No. 2, "The Hunchbacky Man," and No. 6, "Hi Daughter, Ho Daughter."

F15   *Gold Khan*, translated by Norman Cohn, London, 1946.

In his preface (p. 7–8), A.W. lauds the skill and poetic feeling of the translator, "with his power to make us feel that nothing interposes between the reader of these songs and the primordial splendour of Siberian demi-gods." The six legends in the book are selected from Anton Schiefner's German metrical versions of the Turkic traditional songs.

F15a   Sitwell, E. *A Notebook on William Shakespeare*, London, 1948.

Dedicated to A.W. and Beryl de Zoete.

F15b   Herbert, E. [E. H. Kenney], *A Confucian Notebook*, London, 1950.

Brief commendatory half-page foreword by A.W.

F16   Conze, E. *Buddhism, its essence and development*, Oxford [1951].

Preface by A.W. (p. [9]) says that Dr. Conze's comprehensive account is valuable in giving the reader, without distortion of the facts of Buddhism, an emotional and intellectual reaction to them.

F17   "Displacements by a newcomer" in *Times Literary Supplement*, Sept. 18, 1953, p. 597.

Letter to the editor protesting against the attitude of a reviewer who, in an article entitled "Displacements by a newcomer" (Sept. 4, 1953), invited his readers to reconsider their estimate of the work of Edith Sitwell.

The poetess wrote, in a letter to Jack Lindsay, that he and A.W. are the only two people who know what her early poetry means.

F18   Boyce, M. *The Manichaean hymn-cycles in Parthian*, London, 1954.

Acknowledges A.W.'s help with the Chinese text of *Huwīdagman* 1, previously translated by Tsui Chi in *BSOAS*, Vol. XI, 1943–46, p. 199–208.

F18a   [*Letter to the editor*] in *Nine*, April 1956, p. 29.

Answers some points raised by James Liu in a review of **A31** and **A33** in *Nine*, Winter, 1953–54, p. 55–58.

F19   Gray, B. *Buddhist Cave Paintings at Tun-huang*, London, 1959.

A.W. makes some suggestions on points of iconography and epigraphy, in his preface (p. 13–14), "in fulfilment of a promise made before Mr. Gray fortunately undertook to write a text to accompany these plates."

F20   Wu Shih-ch'ang. *On "The Red Chamber Dream,"* Oxford, 1961.

A.W. wrote a foreword (p. vii–viii) to this study of the way in which "a novel is related to the life of the individual (or individuals) who composed it and the process by which his or their experience of life was sublimated into it," and raises a point in connexion with the linguistic identity of the first eighty and the last forty chapters. See also **F8**.

F21   Liu Ts'un-yan. *The Authorship of the "Fêng Shên Yen I,"* Wiesbaden, 1962.

In his preface (p. [I]) A. W. commends the work of Dr. Liu, who attributes the novel to Lu Hsi-hsing.

F22   de Zoete, B. *The Thunder and the Freshness*, London, 1963.

A.W. made this collection of Beryl de Zoete's essays, and in his preface (p. 7–11), quoting from her notes, he gives some information about the de Zoetes.

F23 Bauer, W., and Franke, H. *The Golden Casket,* London, 1965.

Christopher Levenson, who translated this collection of Chinese novellas from the German, records his indebtedness for A.W.'s suggestions and explanations.

F24 Graham, A. C. *Poems of the late T'ang,* Harmondsworth, 1965.

Thanks A.W. for advice and criticism.

F25 Levy, H. S. *Chinese Footbinding,* New York, 1966.

One-page foreword by A.W.

G: SOME APPEARANCES
IN ANTHOLOGIES

G1   French, J. L. *Lotus and Chrysanthemum: An Anthology of Chinese and Japanese Poetry*, New York, 1927.

Contains: p.   3–5   Nos. 63, 62, 59, 57, 56 and 37 of 170.
31–45   Nos. 12, 6, 7, 2 and 4 of *The Temple*.
129–47   Complete text of "Some Poems . . ." (**B21**, *q.v.*), and revisions of some of the verses published in *Japanese Poetry* (**A5**, *q.v.*).
218–20   The major part of Appendix I to *The Temple*.

G2   Tietjens, E. *Poetry of the Orient*, New York, 1928.

Contains: p. 136–66   *Manyō* Nos. 125, 1257, 1796. *Ryōjin Hisshō* Nos. 3, 7, 12 from "Some Poems . . ." (**B21**, *q.v.*). From *Japanese Poetry*, *Manyō* Nos. 741, 778, 905, 1001, 2330. *Kokin* Nos. 525, 548. *Shū-i* No. 848. *Gosen* No. 209. *Rōyei* p. 171. *Zokusensai* No. 397. Hōshi (2), (3) and (5).
199–237   Nos. 1, 6, 12, 15(2), 19, 31, 41, 59, 76, 77, 82, 113, 137, 144 from 170. Nos. 8, 35, 52, 121, 148 from *More Translations*.

G3   Van Doren, M. *An Anthology of World Poetry*, New York, 1928.

Contains: p.   5–48   Nos. 8, 10, 12, 36, 39, 43, 49, 57, 68, 82, 92, 94, 136 of 170.
Nos. 1, 6, 9, 10, 18, 41, 49, 64, 67 of *More Translations*.
Nos. 4, 11, 14 of *The Temple*.

Manyō Nos. 106, 354, 361, 632, 687,
744, 778, 905, 979, 1001, 1179, 1291,
1426, 1500, 1879, 2330, 2375.
Kokin Nos. 147, 158, 169, 481, 525,
560, 637, 797, 895, 961.
Shū-i Nos. 10, 190, 202, 223, 224, 565.
Seven Poems by Saigyo Hōshi, all in
Japanese Poetry.

G4   Untermeyer, L. *Modern British Poetry: A Critical
Anthology,* New York, 1930.

Contains: p. 630–32   No. 51 of *More Translations.*
No. 10 of *The Temple.*
A song from the *Book of Odes* printed
on p. 16 of *An Introduction* . . . (A9).

G5   Yeats, W. B. *The Oxford Book of Modern Verse,
1892–1935,* Oxford, 1936.

Contains: p. 247–56   No. 12 of *The Temple.*

G6   Edwards, E. D. *The Dragon Book,* London, 1938.

Contains: p. 112–18   Nos. 82 and 120 of *170.*
Nos. 23 and 52 of *More Translations.*
Nos. 5 (part) and 10 of *The Temple.*

G6a   Singer, K. *The Life of ancient Japan: selected contemporary texts illustrating social life before the Era of
Seclusion,* Tokyo, 1939.

The editor used extracts from the introduction to *The Nō
Plays, The Pillow-Book* and *The Tale of Genji,* I, II and V.

G7   *Chinese Love Poems,* The Peter Pauper Press, New
York, 1942.

Contains: *passim* Nos. 4, 13–15, 17, 18, 22, 26, 28, 30, 32, 33, 35, 37, 43, 45, 46, 48, 53, 57, 74, 75, 91, 96, 101 (part), 116 (part) of *The Book of Songs*.

G8 Lin Yutang. *The Wisdom of China and India*, New York, 1942.

Contains: p. 892–97 No. 1 of *More Translations*.

G9 Juby, P. *Chinese Poetry*, Pretoria, 1943.

Contains: *passim* Nos. 19, 53, 58, 82, 94, 124 and 145 (1) of *170*.
Nos. 3, 6, 7, 10, 30, 48 and 51 of *More Translations*.

G9a Valensina, G., and Montale, E. *Liriche Cinese*, Torino, 1943.

Of the 167 pieces in the anthology, 140 are drawn from *170* and *More Translations*.

G10 Hsaio Ch'ien. *A Harp with a thousand strings* (*A Chinese anthology in six parts*), London, 1944.

Contains: p. xii   Preface by Arthur Waley.
203–4   No. 37 of *170*.
219   No. 146 of *170*.
314–15   C47.
346–59   The limitations of Chinese Literature. [Reprint of the Introductions to *170* and *The Temple*]

G11 Sitwell, E. *Planet and Glow-worm: a Book for the Sleepless*, London, 1944.

Contains: p. 31–40   Nos. 11 and 18 of *The Nō Plays*.
41   Nos. 19 and 69 of *170*.

G12 Trevelyan, R. C. *From the Chinese*, London, 1945.

Contains: *passim* Nos. 54, 79, 125 and 141 of 170.
Nos. 34, 35, 51 and 64 of *More Translations*.
Nos. 4, 5, 7 and 11 of *The Temple*.
Nos. 56, 160 and 225 of *The Book of Songs*.

G13 Sitwell, E. A *Book of the Winter*, London, 1950.

Contains: p. 1–2   *The Godless Month*, reprinted from *The Tale of Genji*, p. 55–56.

3–4   Nos. 19 and 69 of 170.

43   No. 10 of *The Temple*.

47–48   A passage from *Hachi no Ki*, No. 8 in *The Nō Plays*.

81   No. 130 of 170.

84   *Two Letters*, re-printed from *Blue Trousers*, p. 46 and 154.

G14 Sitwell, E. A *Book of flowers*, London, 1952.

Contains: p. 55   *Two Letters*, re-printed from *Blue Trousers*, p. 46 and 154.

G15 Keene, D. *Anthology of Japanese literature . . .*, New York, 1955.

The volume, dedicated to A.W., forms part of the *UNESCO collection of representative works, Japanese series*.

Contains: p. 106–36   *Yūgao*, re-printed from *The Tale of Genji* (**A11**), p. 92–129.

137–44   Two passages from *The Pillow-book . . .* (**A16**), p. 37–47 and 116–21.

167–69   Six poems from the *Ryōjin Hisshō* (**B21**, 1, 2, 8, 11, 12 and 13).

| 170–76 | *The Lady who loved insects* (**A18**). |
| 286–300 | *Atsumori* and *The Damask Drum* from *The Nō Plays* (**A6**). |

G16 Yohannan, J. D. A *Treasury of Asian literature*, New York, 1956.

Contains: p.	55–89	Chapter V of *The Tale of Genji*.
	240–46	*Atsumori* from *The Nō Plays* . . .
	271–74	*Manyō* Nos. 309, 350, 660, 687, 741, 1001, 1251, 1426, 2375, 3222. *Kokin* Nos. 158, 387, 409, 493, 517, 542, 560, 948, from *Japanese Poetry* . . .

G17 Sitwell, E. *The Atlantic Book of British and American Poetry*, New York, 1958.

Contains: p. 1027–31   Nos. 19, 68, 69, 87, 94 and 130 of 170.
Nos. 4, 10 of *The Temple*.
Anonymous poem on p. 193 of *Chinese Poems*, 1946.

G18 Klemer, D. J. *Chinese Love Poems*, New York, 1959.

Contains: *passim*   Nos. 13, 20, 24, 25, 58, 59, 60, 71 and 72 of 170.

G19 Allott, K. *The Penguin Book of Contemporary Verse* 1918–1960, Harmondsworth, 1962.

Contains: p. 111–12   Nos. 26 and 54 of *More Translations*, reprinted from *Chinese Poems*, 1946.

G20   Birch, C. *Anthology of Chinese Literature* . . . , New York, 1965.

The volume, dedicated to A.W., forms part of the *UNESCO collection of representative works, Chinese series,* and contains material from **A3, 10, 25, 27, 30, 31** and **33**.

G21   Steiner, G. *The Penguin Book of Modern Verse Translation,* Harmondsworth, 1966.

Contains: p. 133–40   Nos. 17 (11), 24, 39, 65, 82 and 87 of 170.
                      Nos. 5 and 10 of *The Temple.*
                      Poems on p. 34 and 76 of *The Poetry and Career of Li Po.*

H: SELECT LIST OF MATERIAL
ON ARTHUR WALEY

The best introduction to Arthur Waley is, of course, to be found in his own writings. Much concerning his attitudes and approach can be learned from the prefaces to his books. He gives a little valuable biographical information in the preface to the second edition of *170 Chinese Poems*, 1962, and Peter Quennell adds some anecdotes in "Literary Letter from London," published in the *New York Times Book Review* of March 4, 1962.

The following brief list could serve as a starting point for study.

[Clutton Brock, A.?] "A New Planet" in *Times Literary Supplement*, Nov. 15, 1917.

Squire, J. "A Translator of Genius," in his *Essays at Large*, 1922.

Bates, E. S. *Modern Translation*, 1936.

Hsieh Wen-tung. "English Translations of Chinese Poetry," in *The Criterion*, April 1938, p. 403–24.

Bates, E. S. *Intertraffic: Studies in Translation*, 1943.

Teele, R. E. *Through a Glass Darkly*, Ann Arbor, 1949.

[Cohen, J. M.?] "Dr. Waley's Translations," in *Times Literary Supplement*, Oct. 20, 1950.

Yashiro, Yukio. "Waley, the Hermit Japanologist" in *Bungei Shunjû*, Dec. 1957, p. 112–19. [*in Japanese*]

[?] "From the Chinese," in *Times Literary Supplement*, Mar. 3, 1961.

Johns, F. A. "A Collection of papers of Arthur Waley and Beryl de Zoete" in *Journal of the Rutgers University Library*, June 1966, p. 59–61.

Morris, I. "Arthur Waley," in *Encounter* [London], Dec. 1966, p. 50–57.

Hawkes, D. "Obituary of Dr. Arthur Waley" in *Asia Major*, N.S. Vol. XII, Pt. 2, 1966, p. 143–47.

INDEX

Book Reviews and Anthologies are not included in the index.

About the Author

Francis A. Johns served for eight years in the Royal Air Force, during which time his stay in China led to a special interest in Chinese culture. He was a librarian in England and Canada before beginning his studies at Rutgers—The State University, where he secured his B.A. and M.A. as well as his degree in librarianship from the Graduate School of Library Service. The author of bibliographical and bibliothecal articles in journals, Mr. Johns in 1965 re-discovered and published the *Chinese Poems* (1916), which nowhere bore Arthur Waley's name as translator. A Fellow of The Library Association (Great Britain) and a member of The Oriental Ceramic Society and The Bibliographical Society of America, he is now University Bibliographer at Rutgers.